JUSTICE FOR MY SON

JUSTICE FOR MY SON

VERA DUFFY
with Martin Duffy ∽

Gill & Macmillan

Gill & Macmillan
Hume Avenue, Park West, Dublin 12
with associated companies throughout the world
www.gillmacmillan.ie

© Vera Duffy 2012
978 07171 5100 4

Typography design by Make Communication
Print origination by O'K Graphic Design, Dublin
Printed in the UK by MPG Books Ltd, Cornwall

This book is typeset in 13/16 pt Minion.

The paper used in this book comes from the wood pulp
of managed forests. For every tree felled, at least one
tree is planted, thereby renewing natural resources.

A CIP catalogue record for this book is available from
the British Library.

5 4 3 2 1

This book was written to honour my dead son Alan, who was robbed of a normal life, and all children affected by vaccines to protect 'the common good'.

The book would not have been possible, especially now that I suffer from multiple sclerosis, if not for my brother-in-law Martin Duffy, whom I now consider to be my special brother. He put hours of patience and dedication into going through thousands of files from various hospitals and picking out relevant points. I will be forever grateful for his dedication to me and to Alan.

CONTENTS

ACKNOWLEDGMENTS   VIII

INTRODUCTION   IX

1.   Kevin   1
2.   The Vaccinations   16
3.   The Association for Vaccine-Damaged Children   34
4.   Renee   60
5.   The Truth   82
6.   Alan   92
7.   Justice   110
8.   Long Battles   125
9.   The Verdict   144
10.   Looking for Meaning   163

AFTERWORD: PRODUCT RECALL   180

HOW ALAN DUFFY DIED   183

BOOKS AND WEBSITES   208

ACKNOWLEDGMENTS

To all those wonderful parents who refused to give up and kept me going with what information they had and who received some form of justice, unlike us here in Ireland:

Celia Young (Dublin)
Jackie Fletcher (JABS, UK)
Meryll Nee (England)
Rosemary Kessick (England)
Rosemary Fox (England)
Barbara Loe Fisher (NVIC, US)
Kathi Williams (NVIC, US)
Congressman Dan Burton (US)
Harris J. Coulter (medical historian)

I will never get the justice I want in my country, but thank you for all you have done for me over the years.

I also want to thank my family and Kevin's family:
My mother, Mary Malone
My sister Anna
Kevin's sisters Brigid Loy, Ethel Carruthers and the late Maureen Gibney.

These were the people who were prepared at any time to take care of Alan for as long as Kevin and I needed when I was nearing breaking point and needed to recharge my batteries. I was always very grateful to know Alan would get the same care from them that I would give him. Thank you all for caring so much.

INTRODUCTION

In September 2008, the Coroner's Court made its final decision on the cause of my son Alan's death. It marked the end of another long battle in my attempt to have the Irish government acknowledge that my son had been brain-damaged by the whooping cough vaccine. I was back in the same court where once, years before, I had to listen to a medical expert say that I had said my son was a 'very odd' child who had never smiled. Now, readers, look at the cover of this book and decide for yourselves.

In July 2008, the HSE—for me, the Eastern Health Board I had done battle with for years—set out its new vaccination programme for Irish children. All the details are there to be downloaded from its impressive website (www.immunisation.ie). That programme dismisses all contra-indications to the vaccine, even those that had, in years gone by, been acknowledged by the Irish medical profession. It does, however, make the extraordinary statement: 'The vaccines used in Ireland are safe. All medicines can cause side effects, but with vaccines these are usually mild, like a sore arm or leg or a slight fever. Serious side effects to vaccines are extremely rare.' I had reached the end of my own journey, seeking justice for my 'extremely rare' deceased son, and was seeing the Irish government set itself back at the drug company-friendly position it had adapted in the 1950s. If you are caught in one place for long enough, the world comes back around to you.

Getting Alan's case through the Coroner's Court took 12½ years because the State had to fight with everything they could throw at us. Every time the coroner, Brian Farrell, went near the topic of vaccine damage to Alan, he was slapped with a judicial review: first to the High Court, where he lost his case. The coroner then asked to be 'indemnified'—that the State would pay his costs—for his appeal to the Supreme Court. The judge refused, thinking this would stop the coroner. That did not happen. The coroner used his own funds to make his appeal to the Supreme Court and he would not allow me to help him financially.

We lost. Old Coroner's laws had to be applied which say that the coroner is not allowed to lay blame for the cause of a death; only where, when and how death occurred. I always felt that the coroner knew the truth of what happened to my son. When we met first, I remember telling him: 'The State will never let you say what happened.' His reply was: 'I am the coroner and I can only tell the truth.' How wrong he was. As the years of legal battle continued he was, you could call it, gagged.

It was about six years into that legal battle when I was diagnosed with chronic multiple sclerosis. Where was God? I had long ago lost all faith in the medical profession. In my experience, I had come to the conclusion that none of the doctors who had treated Alan would admit what had happened to him. Put it to you this way—how could they? One life means nothing. Only the herd.

One remark I will never forget was a Supreme Court judge saying, 'Can these things really harm people?' Even they didn't know.

So now here I am. My son was destroyed by something that was meant to protect him. My daughter Renee died of a tumour. I screamed at God with anger. I had had enough. I deserved justice.

I buried a skeleton. Alan was born perfectly normal. Then he was taken from me and I couldn't help him. There were times when I was very sorry for him. He had my utmost respect. But no one could blame me for my lack of respect for the medical profession. Nothing could be done for Renee, Alan, and now me.

Sometime during the inquest, after the Supreme Court ruling, I was sent papers of damning information from a very reliable source on the headed notepaper of a pharmaceutical company. There it all was in front of me: very serious reactions to their pertussis vaccine; details of batch numbers, reaction times, extreme reactions such as paralysis, convulsions, encephalitis . . . death. This was very real. It was the result of research done by the pharmaceutical company at a time when the public were being told that the most extreme reactions to vaccines were swollen arms or irritability.

I, of course, handed these documents to the coroner. It made no difference. He still could not bring it up in court. So my husband Kevin and I had this information, but it could not be spoken about. Meanwhile, in the Coroner's Court there was a representative from the pharmaceutical company present every day writing down a report on the proceedings.

So let's go back to the Coroner's Court. What was the coroner to do in this case? He couldn't direct a jury because he couldn't mention vaccines. So what was he to say? On that day in September 2008, I sat waiting for the coroner's final verdict. My family and I had been exhausted by this circus—12½ years of it. The coroner looked down at me and I could read his thoughts. When he was about to close and give his decision, I walked out. I did so for two reasons: I knew it would be easier for him to say what he had to say without seeing me. I also did it for myself. I did not want to hear what he was about to say.

On New Year's Eve 1995 my son Alan died. He was 22 years of age, but his life ended when he was five months old. I have spent 30 years seeking justice for him, and it has turned my life into one long battle. People tell me to leave it alone—that Alan is dead now and let him rest. But I cannot do that. I would feel I was abandoning my child and that I would be letting the State get away with killing him. I owe it to my children, to my husband and to myself to keep on searching for proof of what I know caused Alan's death.

I also believe that Alan is not at rest and will not be at rest until his story is told and the cause of his death is proven. I am writing this book for him and for my family. I am writing in the hope that somehow those who know the truth will tell it or be forced to tell it. I am hoping, too, that other people with similar stories will come forward—as they did a long time ago when I set up the Irish Association for Vaccine-Damaged Children—and add new pressure to get to the truth.

I am not against vaccination; I am against ignorance. I am against the Irish government's policy of hiding the faults and risks in its vaccination programme. The children being vaccinated have no voice. When Alan was a child I was, like most parents, ignorant of the dangers. We trusted the medical profession; yet I think that in the past they were just as ignorant of the truth as we were. I believe that the government and the pharmaceutical companies keep a lot from doctors. Yet the doctors are the ones dealing with people at the front line if something goes wrong. I've never sought to blame a doctor for what happened to Alan, but I won't rest until the medical profession and the Irish government acknowledge what happened to him.

This book, however, will also reveal the lies the pharmaceutical companies told. For the first time, the documents I received from medical sources in Britain will be presented here. That evidence was the last straw in scaring the British government into setting up a compensation and support system for vaccine-damaged children. I am now ready to launch that time bomb here in Ireland.

———

I have written this book for all new mums out there. Never trust what you are told about vaccines. Check everything first. The information is all there for you now. What happened to Alan could happen again, and then the cover-up will begin again in this country of leprechauns and liars. Enjoy every moment of your child's life. They are there out of the love of two people and are part of you both. Our children are precious to us, and not simply part of a 'herd'. Every life is precious and irreplaceable. It is your responsibility to take care of them. That means you should check and ask questions. Then make an informed decision. Your baby has no voice and no choice—their welfare is up to you.

This book is the story of my life—a life lived in the shadow of a tragedy that could have been avoided. It is the story of my battle to see justice done for my lost son. It is the story of how I have struggled to understand why God chose such a difficult path through life for me. It is also the story of a life blessed with the love of a wonderful husband and family.

Chapter 1 ∿

| KEVIN

Did you know that you are part of a herd? I learned that with mass vaccination programmes the population is referred to by that name. The herd I was born into is Irish. As the newly independent country was getting on its feet, housing estates were built to the north and south of Dublin to clear people out of the inner city tenements. I grew up in one such estate on the northside. The love of my life grew up in one on the southside.

I was born and raised in a two-up two-down house in Cabra, a working-class housing estate. My father, Felix Malone, died suddenly when I was 10 years old. He was surveying work on the roof of a market building when the roof collapsed under him. When he died, my mother was left with six children to raise, the youngest of us 11 months old and the eldest 12 years old. I would say that we were poverty-stricken: a 36-year-old woman left alone to raise six children in 1950s Ireland. I remember the Saint Vincent de Paul coming to us at Christmas to give us presents and I remember my Mam knitting things for us as Christmas presents. Our toys were things like broken crockery. When our shoes wore down we put cardboard in them. We were close to being taken from our mother and put into the institutions that now the world knows were hell-holes of abuse.

My mother was a great woman to hold on to us. The authorities tried to convince her to let some of us go, but she would not do it. She also never considered marrying again. As she told me many years later, "I couldn't bear the thought of some other man chastising Felix's kids." Along with the burden of raising us, Mam also had to find work. She told us once that she had a job in the Pillar Café on O'Connell Street. I was proud of her and wanted to go visit her in her job. I expected to find her there working as a waitress. Instead, when I went there I found that she was working in the basement, cleaning the toilets and gathering the coins paid for the use of the latrines. When I saw her there I went out on to O'Connell Street and I roared crying. She did all that for us.

We got food dockets and I was given the job of collecting food for the family. The food was given out in steel buckets and I, being proud, would cover these with scarves as I walked home with them.

There was some small insurance payment given for my father's death which was controlled by the courts. My Mam would have to go to the courts every time she needed something for us: for Confirmation or Communion and so on. The woman had extraordinary strength to keep us together. For all that we went through, my brothers and sisters and I grew up as decent people who never turned to crime or violence. I thank my mother's strength for that.

Each of us in turn, as soon as we were finished primary school, went to work. When I was 14 my mother took me out to find me a job. She marched me into Fennessy's shoe shop on Dorset Street and asked the manageress there if I could have a job as an apprentice. The woman agreed. I didn't want to work in a shoe shop, but no one was asking my opinion. Still, I had a job and I was earning money—nearly all of which, of course, went to my mother—and as far as I was concerned I was an adult.

When I started work at the shop I discovered there was a general manager over all the Fennessy shoe shops around the city. I saw this gorgeous blue Zodiac car pull up outside the shop with loads of badges on its front grill, and out stepped this young man who was tall and good looking. I thought to myself, he's drop-dead gorgeous. This was Kevin Duffy. He was always dressed immaculately in lovely suits, and even though he was only a teenager, he was already a boss. He would always walk into the shop and find something wrong or he'd want to know what was selling and why was something else not selling. He was very serious, and I found out that he had gone to be a Christian Brother and that he was very shy. He was from a family of 13 who lived in a working-class housing estate in Crumlin on the southside of Dublin. The minute I clapped eyes on Kevin I was madly in love with him and I knew I was going to marry him.

Soon I was out to get my man. In those days, shoe shops were set out with boxes stacked up high over the display racks. I used to say to the other girls in the shop, "If you see his car pulling up, call me." They would call me and I would immediately climb a ladder so he could have a good look at my legs. But Kevin only had his mind on business and I was getting nowhere.

"You shouldn't be so high up that ladder. You might fall," is all he'd say.

Time went by and I was making no progress. Then I was moved to the Fennessy shop on Talbot Street. One time I was dressed up like a Geisha as part of some sales promotion. I had the photograph out for Kevin to see and asked him if he liked it. He just grunted that he did and went off about his work.

Later, another girl working in the shop, who was friends with Kevin, told me, "I think he fancies you."

"You'd never think it," I said. "Do you think he'd ask me out?"

"I think he's shy and afraid you'd say no," she said.

"Well listen," I said, "if you can find a way of talking to him about it, tell him 'if you ask, I think she'll say yes.'"

This girl came back to me a few days later. "He's afraid of his life to ask you out because he thinks you'll say no. He's never gone out with a girl before. You're the first girl he's ever thought of going out with."

So a couple of days later I was in the staff room and Kevin came in. He gathered up his courage and asked me would I go out with him.

"I don't know," I said. "I'd have to ask my Mammy."

"Oh." He was shocked. "Right then."

Nothing more happened because I really did think I should ask my mother, but I didn't know how to ask her. But then fate took over. I was upstairs in the stockroom of the shop—not because I needed to do anything, but because Kevin was there, and so I pretended I had work to do there. He was on one side of the shelves and I was on the other. He was working and I was pretending to be working. All of a sudden the wooden floor collapsed under me. I fell through the boards, screaming, and if I hadn't put my hands out I would have gone through the floor. Kevin ran around and grabbed me. My leg caught a nail and there was a long rip up along it—shaped like a seven by the way I fell.

Kevin lifted me up and my leg was pouring blood. All I could think, though, was, this is great. He's going to take me to the hospital. He brought me to the Mater Hospital, where I was bandaged up and taken care of. On the way back, in his car, he asked me if I would go to the pictures with him. I said I would.

The first film we ever went to see was an Elvis Presley film at the Capitol cinema. When we went in, we were ushered to the back row and I was shocked because I knew that that was where couples kissed. And more—all kinds of things went on in the back row.

"I'm not sitting in the back row," I said.

The usher shone the torch around. "There's nowhere else to sit." So we sat in the back row and watched Elvis. Nothing else happened.

Kevin and I started going out together and I was absolutely nuts about him. At the same time I worried that I liked him too much and that I was too young to be feeling so strongly about someone. After a while I decided to go out with other fellas. I started being free and single again. I'd go off on holidays with the girls. Kevin was still there, of course, because we worked together. I would do the most awful things. I'd go off dancing with the girls at the Television Club on Harcourt Street behind his back and I would date other fellas. Then I would go into town a few nights later and there would be fellas stationed at different places along O'Connell Street, all expecting me to show up for a date. I'd arrive in town on the bus with my friend Sylvia Morris and I'd be showing her these fellas waiting. "Which one will I go out with?" I'd ask her. Usually I'd leave them all standing there and go off to the Television Club again with Sylvia. None of the fellas was ever a patch on Kevin. Sylvia met Kevin and she said he was gorgeous and I was crazy.

"I know I'll marry him," I said. "It doesn't matter how many fellas I go out with. I'm just too young now."

But the time came when Kevin had had enough. He called it off. I couldn't believe it—that anyone would dare give me a dose of my own medicine! I was broken-hearted. I tried everything to convince him to go out with me again, but he had made up his mind. I then heard he was going out with another girl. I felt completely gutted. None of the fellas I had gone out with meant anything. All I wanted to do was to avoid getting serious so young, but I couldn't bear to think of life without Kevin.

One night I knew he had gone into town on a date with this girl to see a film. Sylvia and I walked around town until we found his car, and we reckoned from where it was parked that he was most likely at either the Carlton or—across O'Connell Street from the Carlton—the Savoy. We watched the people coming out of the Savoy and he wasn't among them. We ran across the road and I hid in a telephone box and the two girls who were with me scouted for me.

"We see him," Sylvia said.

"Is he with a girl?"

"There's some woman with him."

"Jesus! Is she holding his hand?"

"Vera, she's linking him!"

"Oh my God!" That was it for me. I was going to get him back, and I was never going to treat him badly again. I found out afterwards that he was afraid of his life of the woman he was out with that time, because she was so serious and wanted him to meet her parents. He was glad to be back with someone who wasn't trying to grab on to him. We went on dating after that, still having troubles from time to time, but never doubting that we would always be together. Kevin is and was the only man I ever wanted. It was only always him. He's handsome, kind and a great family man. One thing that attracted me to him from early on is the fact that he doesn't drink. When I was out dancing and seeing other men, if a man had a smell of drink off him it would remind me of my father and that would be the end of it. I was glad that Kevin would never smell of drink. He was also always hard-working and ambitious. He wasn't afraid to take risks, and I admired him for that. He opened his own shoe shop eventually and was devoted to building a good future for us.

Relationships in those days were different. Kevin and I were a couple for years, but there was no question that we would be allowed to go away on a holiday together. There was certainly no question that we would sleep together. The best privacy we could get for a coort was in Kevin's car or else babysitting his little brother Martin on Saturday nights. With the luxury of a couch in Kevin's home, to get Martin out of the way we'd send him to the shops for messages—lemonade and ice cream.

We got engaged on my 21st birthday. We were married when I was 23. Typical of Kevin, he wouldn't close the shops he owned for a wedding on a Saturday, so we got married on a Wednesday, which was a half-day. I had the dressmaker get a corset for me because I insisted on having an 18 inch waist on my wedding day, so that Kevin could fit his hands around my waist. On my wedding day, as I was about to leave the house and with the limousine waiting outside, I took one last look at myself in the mirror and decided that I didn't like my head-dress. With everyone going hysterical in the house, I took off the head-dress, got a needle and thread and changed it to something simpler that I liked better.

Kevin and I went to Paris for our honeymoon. We were two innocents in every respect. We couldn't figure out if the bidet in our hotel room was for washing your feet or for having a pee.

———

From the start of our marriage we rented a house in Moatfield Road, Coolock. I was anything but a domesticated housewife. When we came back from our honeymoon, we were surrounded by all the gorgeous wedding gifts I had asked for—like silk sheets and beautiful vases—but we had to boil eggs in the kettle until Kevin went out and bought a set of pots.

A year after our marriage, our daughter Tracey was born. The delivery took 16 hours and I was in agony. In those days the men were sent home and so I was alone in all this misery. By the time Tracey was born, I was in a terrible state. The doctor afterwards said it probably should have been a Caesarean section, but this had been realised too late. Instead, it was what was called a high forceps delivery. Tracey was a 10 lb baby and I was too small. When I came home I was very ill and soon got a bad kidney infection. I was taken back into hospital. When I got home again I became very depressed. At that time Kevin was working very long hours running his shoe shops. So I was alone at home with a new baby and feeling terrible. I was, of course, suffering from postnatal depression. But in those days the medical profession had no name for it and no compassion for its victims.

I would sit crying all day long, being stuck there minding this little baby. I was in my little suburban house in Coolock and I felt lost. The phone would ring and I wouldn't answer it. I would just stare out the window. Finally, one night when Kevin came home, I said, "Do you know what I did today? I put Tracey outside the front door in the pram and then I turned on the gas in the oven. I sat there waiting to see how long it would take until I died."

In truth I had done nothing of the kind. But saying so seemed to be one sure way of getting his attention. What I needed was understanding and help. We were just two kids, and we had no one to advise us. I didn't know what I was doing or what saying such things could lead to.

Kevin decided that we should go back to the doctor at Mount Carmel where Tracey was born. I told this doctor that I was alone at home all day, crying and not seeing any sense in what life was all about. The doctor gave me the name of a place he thought I should go to for the weekend.

"Where's that?" I asked.

"It's in Blackrock."

I had no idea what kind of place he was talking about, but I felt happier because I was finally getting attention. When I got there I found out that it was a psychiatric home run by an order of nuns. Kevin and I sat in the reception, and a nun sat with us and took all my details. As I looked around, I was no longer feeling so happy about the attention I was getting. How could I turn all this around?

"How long am I going to be here?" I asked the nun.

"We'll hold on to you for maybe a day or two," she said.

I was then brought to a psychiatrist who started talking to me about my childhood. He asked me about my father, Felix Malone. I told him that I hadn't known my father very well and that I was mostly raised by my grandmother. My father was a heavy drinker, as were most men in those days. One of our jobs was to go to the pub and get him home safely. He had a bike, and our Mam was afraid he'd have an accident on the way home if he'd had too much drink. We might have to hide in doorways to watch out for him and pick him up if he fell.

He was in England for several years—from before I was born until I was 3 years old. There was no work in Ireland at the time. My mother told me that when he saw me for the first time he said to her, "Get that snotty-nosed young one out of here."

"That's Vera," she said.

"Oh, you mean that's mine?" He thought I was some neighbour's child.

In a strange way, the distance between him and me saved me. I never bonded with him, nor he with me. So when he was in one of his rages over something one of us might have done, he would line up my brothers and sisters and beat them, but he always set me aside in a corner. I remember one night I was asleep and he woke me. His mother was a dressmaker and had given him some clippings of material to give me. But he had been in a fight on the way home—when he was drunk he'd get in a fight with God himself—and he was covered in blood and dirt, and so were the pieces of cloth he was giving me.

"They're all dirty," I said.

He just threw them at me. But I suppose the thought was there. He was bringing something home for me.

One of my most vivid childhood memories of him is of sitting on the stairs listening to him downstairs in a rage, breaking things. He never hit our mother, but she told me that she used to lock herself in the bathroom and sleep there to avoid having sex with him.

He died in the roof accident and, in those days, children were not allowed to attend funerals. I remember we five youngest children sitting on the wall of our front garden watching the hearse with our father pass on its way from the church to the cemetery. I remember we waved at the coffin.

"Do you feel responsible for your father's death?" the psychiatrist asked me.

"I don't feel responsible," I said.

When I told the psychiatrist all this, I think he decided I was going to be there for more than a day or two. They gave me some kind of medication that knocked me into Kingdom Come and turned the next two weeks into a blur. They put me into a horrible little room with a little bed, a formica wardrobe and bars on the window. Kevin had been sent away. They told him that I needed this treatment and that it was for my own good because I had considered taking my own life. The lie I had told to get attention had come back to haunt me.

Either they lowered the dose or I began to get used to it, but I started to come more to my senses and realise the situation I was in. Instead of trying to be well behaved to be let go, though, I started behaving even worse. My opinion was, if they think I'm mad, I might as well act mad. I would for instance go into the chapel of the home and turn all the statues back to front, or put one of my bras on a statue. One of the jobs they used to give us was to wash the sheets in the baths. It was revolting. A lot of patients were incontinent and wet their beds. I would let the water overflow and flood the bathrooms. I was caught doing this one day and was given a bucket and mop and told to clean it all up. I had lingerie among my clothes there, so I went off and put on this see-through négligée and red panties and cleaned up the bathrooms dressed like that.

There was a room for table tennis. We would play, but our aim was to hit all the balls out the window. Then I'd tell the nuns we couldn't play because there were no balls. We'd finally convince the nuns to let us go gather the balls. That was our only chance to get out into the fresh air.

I refused to eat in the dining rooms. I couldn't bear to see all the poor souls there slobbering over their food. I told the nuns to bring my food to my room and they refused, so I said I wouldn't eat at all. When they saw that I was serious, they brought my meals to my room. But if I didn't like the food I wouldn't eat it. One day a nun tried to force me to eat food I didn't like, forcing my mouth open to ram food in. I spat the food out and then threw the tray at the window.

I came to hate the nuns. I became convinced, also, that two of them were lesbians. There was a woman patient I had become friends with and I told her this. "What's a lesbian?" she asked me. When the nuns noticed that I was regularly chatting with this woman, they had her moved to a different part of the institution. But my suspicions about these nuns were raised even more one time when one of them came to me while I was knitting a jumper for myself. I was holding the work I had done so far up to my chest to judge how I was progressing, and she ran her hands over my chest very slowly—pretending to be admiring the knitting.

I heard that Bishop Eamon Casey—a man who years later had to leave his diocese when it was revealed he had a son—was coming to visit the home. The nuns had us all polishing and cleaning everywhere in preparation for the visit. I couldn't bear the way all this fuss was being made just because a bishop was visiting. When he arrived, he was in a room talking with some nuns. I walked in dressed in my negligée and with a banana between my legs. All I wanted to do, trapped in this place, was make a mockery of these people who were trying to control me.

But then something happened that snapped me out of this stupid game. One day I had a phone call from Kevin saying he would be delayed coming to visit me. He had been in a slight car accident and Tracey, in her carrycot in the back seat of the car, had fallen on to the floor of the car. He had taken her to the hospital and she was fine, but the hospital wanted to keep her overnight just to be sure. All I could think was that I had to see Tracey for myself to make sure she was well. I decided I would dress up as a visitor and escape. All our clothes had been taken from us, but I had become friends with a woman there who helped me find some. I wore a scarf to cover my face as much as possible. When all the visitors were leaving, I mixed in with them. We patients had no money, and I had to get from Blackrock to Crumlin—a journey of more than half an hour in a car.

I was still on medication and so I wasn't able to think clearly. I was watching out for Kevin's car—he was driving a white Rover then—and I was wandering out on to the street trying to wave down any car I thought might be Kevin's. A car pulled in and at last I thought I had help. It was the psychiatrist.

"Where are you going, Vera?" he asked. The alarm had been raised shortly after I escaped and people were out looking for me. I pleaded with him to take me to Crumlin to see Tracey, but he refused. I was crying but he wouldn't listen. He dragged me into the car and took me back to the home. There, I was strapped into a bed, my arms and ankles tied to the bed.

"Just let me see that my daughter is okay," I was pleading. But they still refused.

Kevin came and he saw the state I was in. He demanded that the straps be taken off me, but they refused. He eventually convinced them to at least let my hands free and a nun spent the night with me to make sure I didn't try to escape or hurt myself. Kevin promised me that Tracey was fine. But all I could think of was getting out of that place and back to my family and my home.

They would let me out sometimes. Kevin picked me up one Sunday evening and we went for a meal together and then to the Adelphi cinema on Abbey Street. We saw the Richard Harris film *A Man called Horse*, which was very depressing. I didn't want to go back to the 'home', but Kevin said we had to keep our promise. I pleaded with him to take me home, but he said he couldn't. When we got back to the institution they had to drag me from the car to get me back in.

Kevin thought about what had happened and after talking with my family he decided that this was the wrong thing for me. He made up his mind to get me out. Within days, forms were signed and I was free to leave. Told at the start that I needed to be there for a couple of days, I had been there for over a month. The whole thing had been caused by postnatal depression. I craved attention but didn't know how to admit that. The people dealing with me, and people like me at that time, saw me as a problem and not as a person. It was my first taste of how uncaring the 'carers' in the medical profession could be.

―――

A few months later I brought Tracey for her vaccinations at the local health clinic. After the first vaccination, Tracey was screaming. Nevertheless, the doctors went ahead and gave her the second and third set of injections in the following months. Tracey developed a turn in one of her eyes and needed corrective glasses and at times a patch. She ultimately needed three operations to correct the problem. Years later I was told that there was a very likely connection between the vaccinations and Tracey's eye problem. But back in the days of her childhood, we knew nothing of the dangers and troubles that lay ahead.

Kevin and I loved family life. Sundays were special because it was Kevin's one day off and we would all dress up. He adored Tracey and she adored him. When I dressed her on Sunday mornings, she would then want to go into our bedroom, where Kevin was in bed reading the newspapers, to show him her dress and do twirls for him.

Kevin always made a big thing about Christmas. It was a time when he would splash out on all kinds of treats for us. By Christmas 1972 we had something extra to celebrate—I was pregnant again. Kevin was working very hard and his shops were doing well. We were starting to get on in life.

On 11 May 1973, I gave birth to our son Alan in Mount Carmel Hospital. Unlike my experience with Tracey, Alan's delivery was easy. The usual examinations and tests were carried out on Alan when he was born, including the 'heel test', and he had the highest possible score. I still have the hospital records from that time. The pregnancy and delivery were normal, and Alan was in perfect health. He was a happy baby who settled easily after having his bottle. I also had no problems after his birth. We left the hospital after the usual few days and came home to the typical excitement of a new baby. Kevin was delighted to have a son.

When I gave Alan his bath in the morning, he would grip my little fingers with his hands and his grip was very strong. I remember a nurse telling me that if I let his feet touch something solid, I would see his walking reflex. I did this occasionally. It was fun to watch.

Alan was a lovely little baby. The evening time was always the best time. His eyes would be open wide and he would be watching everything. From the time I brought him home until his first check-up, he was always hungry and he always woke for his night feed.

I brought Alan to the Coombe Hospital for his six-week development check. I remember the day well. I had knitted a purple outfit for him and I remember undressing him so the paediatrician could do the tests. Alan was very giggly that day and was having fun doing the tests. The doctor confirmed that Alan was 100 per cent healthy.

My brother Leonard was staying with us around that time and can remember Alan holding his bottle himself from an early age. Leonard recalled one particular incident when Alan was about six weeks old. My brother had noticed that the bottle had fallen out of Alan's mouth and was about to go to him to put it back in, when Alan grabbed the bottle himself in his hands and hooshed it back into his mouth so he could carry on drinking.

"He's been here before," Leonard joked.

By about the age of two and a half months, Alan loved to be on the floor on his tummy. I'd lie on the floor playing with him and he would screech with laughter. He was getting to know my voice, too, and would look around to see where I was. He would chuckle when I played 'peep' around the hood of his pram.

My mother used to call Alan 'smiler' because he was so quick to respond with a smile. She would play on the floor with him too. By the age of about three and a half months Alan was starting to roll over. We would put things in front of him and he would stretch forward and grab them. It was great fun to play with him and tire him out for bed. He was starting to make sounds and to laugh out loud.

The district nurse who came to check on us was very pleased with how Alan was developing. In all her visits she was happy with his development. Her usual parting remark was "Your baby is doing very well. Just keep doing what you're doing." I am absolutely certain that, contrary to what she would write in a report two years later when the controversy about Alan started growing, she never asked me about my family's medical history.

That's the way it was for us back then. Kevin was doing well, we were a happy family, Tracey was growing, and our baby son Alan was thriving. The difficulties I had had after Tracey's birth were far behind me, and I was the mother and wife in a family worlds apart from the one in which I had grown up. I loved the stability and the joys of our family.

When Alan was five months old, I received a note in the post for an appointment to go to the local health centre. It was time for the first of Alan's three-in-one vaccine injections. This vaccine was given at intervals of two months starting when a baby was five months old. The district nurse's notes from around that time state about Alan: 'Visited frequently and infant found to be progressing normally.'

The events of the coming months would change the rest of our lives.

Chapter 2 ∽

| THE VACCINATIONS

On 17 October 1973, I wheeled my five-month-old son up to the local Eastern Health Board clinic. I was like any good mother. I was doing what was best for my child. My mother came with me for company.

We arrived at the Edenmore clinic along with about 20 other mothers and their babies. When it came to Alan's turn, I was called by the nurse at the desk. I was asked my child's name and whether it was his first injection. I was asked no questions about his medical history. I was given a card with Alan's name and the date for his second injection—two months from then. I moved along with the queue of mothers and babies to the doctor.

I told this doctor—a man—that my daughter Tracey had been ill and upset after her vaccinations and the doctor said that if that happened with Alan I should give him aspirin or Calpol. Alan was then given the first of his three-in-one vaccination injections against diphtheria, typhoid and pertussis (whooping cough). He was also given the sugar lump containing the polio vaccination.

As I would later learn, there were contra-indications for the vaccination, and these were listed on the packaging. At the medical centre, however, these were ignored. My record should have shown there was epilepsy in my family—my sister and my cousin have epilepsy. No one noted, and I was not told, that this was a major reason why Alan should not have the pertussis part of the vaccination. The vaccination used then actually introduced a level of meningitis into the system for the body to react to. That's what created the immunity to whooping cough. But for some babies that process is too risky. No one said any of this to me at the time.

I would also later learn that according to written Eastern Health Board procedure I should have been informed of the possible dangers and given the free choice to have only the diphtheria and typhoid vaccinations as opposed to the full combination. I was offered no such option. There was no sign in the medical centre providing information or warnings. I received no information from the nurse or the doctor. I was just another working-class mother on the factory line with another baby to be vaccinated for the good of the herd. It was a different time—for me and for the country—when people in authority were never questioned. We were expected to obey them, and they were trusted to know what was best for us.

A year and a half later this doctor wrote a very different version of that first vaccination from the events as I recall them: 'As customary I questioned the mother and received no adverse answers and certainly I was told of no family history of Epilepsy. In consequence of no adverse conditions being told to me, I proceeded with the inoculations.'

I went home that day feeling I was being a good mother doing what was best for my child. The day went by like any other, and that night Alan slept with no trouble. Later, I would feel as if someone had taken my son away that night and replaced him with another child.

Next day I was downstairs while Alan was having a nap. He let out a sudden scream and I rushed up to him. I picked him up and tried to soothe him, without success. Finally I gave him Calpol, but this didn't settle him either. I didn't understand his distress and it took a long time for him to go back to sleep.

Alan had always been a good feeder and he loved his food. But in the days after the first injection he started throwing up his milk. One day, a few days after that first injection, Alan was lying in his cot when he suddenly began to shake. His eyes rolled in his head and his arms shot straight out. His skin turned grey. I was terrified. I had never seen him like this before. His upset passed, and while I couldn't imagine what was wrong, I was glad he was settling again. But this very same behaviour happened again and again that day—the shaking, turning grey, his eyes rolling. I phoned my local GP, Dr Frank Dwane. Another doctor came out to the house. This doctor said that Alan was teething and also that he had a throat infection. He prescribed an antibiotic.

In the days that followed, when I played with Alan I knew something had changed. He didn't laugh any more; he didn't look at me when I called him; he had lost interest in his surroundings. I remember thinking, where is he going?

The district nurse came by and I told her my concerns. I said that Alan seemed to be losing the will to sit up. She told me I probably wasn't letting Alan sit on the floor enough and in her own notes wrote: 'Infant sitting in pram with pillows and support.' The nurse also told me that Alan might not be feeling well because he was teething. I felt there was more to it than that. He didn't seem to be as alert as before. In the past, when I appeared at the pram looking in at him, he would become excited and smile. This stopped. He paid no attention to me. If he was on the floor and I called him, he didn't respond. It was as if he didn't hear me. Could this all be put down to teething? That's what I was being told.

That wasn't the only change happening. By this time, home life had become miserable and difficult because Kevin had lost his business and we were in a bad financial state. Christmas was approaching and we were facing it penniless, while almost every other day I was constantly calling the doctor out to Alan.

On 12 December I brought Alan to the medical centre for his second injection. When it came to my turn in the queue to see the doctor, I told her that Alan had been unwell after the first injection—having these attacks and throwing up his feeds. I also said—hoping this would postpone the injection—that Alan had a cold. The doctor checked Alan's chest and said he was fine. The second injection was given and I was assured that his little troubles were nothing to worry about.

When I got home, Alan was very quiet and he slept as usual. The next day, however, he was having bouts of twitching and he was throwing up his feed. But this time everything seemed more intense. In the second and third days after the injection, the attacks were not only more frequent but they were more severe. I was becoming very frightened for him.

The only consolation for me was that I knew Alan was due for a major check-up with the paediatrician at the clinic within weeks and my hope was that these strange symptoms would be explained.

So a few weeks later, at the start of January 1974, I was back at the Edenmore clinic to see Dr Neil O'Doherty, the paediatrician, for Alan's routine developmental check-up. I told him about the symptoms, and the doctor examined him. He did simple tests like putting a rattler in front of Alan, testing his reflexes and rolling him on the floor. One test he did was to lift him up by the heels. Alan did not react to being lowered upside down. O'Doherty said this showed Alan had no 'parachute reflex'. I asked him what he thought.

"Alan has a problem," he said.

"What problem?"

"I don't know yet. We never label children that young."

He arranged another appointment for six weeks later, and told me to tell him again about the tremors at the next meeting as they could be important.

When I got home from that appointment, I was very worried. I phoned Dr Corry, who had delivered Alan, and he said that Alan was a perfectly healthy baby at birth and there couldn't be a problem with him. He said there were reasons why a baby might be in some way retarded—a genetic problem or a lack of oxygen at birth or some such clear circumstance—but these would have been evident from birth and did not apply to Alan. Healthy-born babies don't suddenly show signs of retardation at six months, he assured me. I tried not to worry so much about my child, but I still knew something was wrong.

A week after my appointment with O'Doherty, the district nurse came round. She later noted of this visit: 'Infant not sitting alone—falling to one side—not grasping objects or taking anything in his hand.'

I was looking at Alan and asking Kevin could Alan be deaf. He just wasn't responding or acting the way he used to. Sometimes I would see him sitting quietly and then his arms would suddenly jerk out with his hands springing back towards his face. His eyes would roll in his head and he would become ashen-faced. These weren't convulsions and they lasted just a few seconds. I wondered if it was his temper, but he wasn't reacting to anything. He continued to throw up his food. After a meal he would have a bout of projectile vomiting. I used to lay out newspapers all around the kitchen floor after feeding Alan as I knew what to expect.

All the usual infant troubles such as colic were suspected. I was told that Alan's illness was just a part of infancy and I shouldn't worry so much. He had been perfectly healthy and no one had expressed any doubt that he was anything other than a normal baby going through what any child might go through. Doctors didn't share my worries, so who was I to say anything was seriously wrong? It was unimaginable that medicine—something given to you for the good of your health—could do any harm. I was like any other mother at the time. I believed in medicine as a caring profession, and I didn't question what I was being told. They were, after all, beyond being questioned. At the time of the vaccinations I wasn't aware of any possible dangers and if any medic knew of such dangers, they were not pointing them out to me.

The third injection was due on 6 February 1974. Alan had been so unwell after the first and second vaccines that when I went back the third time I tried to avoid his having another injection. I told the doctor—the same woman who had given the second injection—that Alan had been very upset after the other injections, and that he wasn't fit enough for the vaccination. It's not that I was afraid of another vaccination. I said this because I knew another vaccination meant more sleepless nights and I wanted to spare myself that. I didn't want to be put through this poor child screaming again. I was only thinking of myself. I didn't know what the vaccine was doing. I still couldn't imagine there was a connection between the vaccinations and Alan's illness.

The doctor told me that Alan would be worse off if the course of vaccines was not completed. What was I to do? I trusted the doctor. I trusted the medical profession. I did what I was told. Alan was given the third injection. That, I believe, is the one that destroyed him.

A year later, when this doctor—Maire Kennedy—gave her statement about the second and third vaccinations she gave Alan, she wrote:

> As standard practice, prior to immunising the child the mother was asked on both occasions:
> a) was the baby all right after the first/second immunisations or was there any reaction? No reaction reported on either occasion.
> b) was the baby well at the time? Yes. Baby appeared well. Immunisation given.

That was definitely not my own recollection of events. It also isn't supported by Alan's 'Child Health Service pre-school Card' which covers the first year of Alan's life. Nothing has been written in under the headings 'relevant family history' and 'genetic history'. Although the dates of the first two immunisations are noted on the card, the date of the third is not. Written into this card, however, are O'Doherty's notes from 3 January check-up listing his concerns.

As I would later learn, there were several warning signs ignored. The most telling of these, I discovered years later, was a directive issued *the month before* this third vaccination by the deputy Chief Medical Officer from the Immunisation Section and addressed to 'Each immunisation doctor and all members of the Immunisation Staff'. The directive stated:

Any infant who has ever had a convulsion should not be vaccinated against whooping cough until it is two years of age . . . Neurological complications occasionally follow Pertussis vaccine. If you learn that after a previous injection the child was unnaturally limp or drowsy, or had a convulsion or any other sign of Encephalopathy, a further injection must not be given . . .

Such knowledge was years of battle away from me. A medical expert once told me that giving Alan the first injection was an unfortunate mistake by the medics; giving him the second injection was careless; and giving him the third was criminal.

On the way home from the third vaccination, Alan started screeching in the pram—the noise was somewhere between a high-pitched scream and a grunt. I would later learn to recognise that sound as the start of a convulsion, but I didn't know it then. I looked in at him in the pram wondering if he had thrown up. He hadn't. I rushed home as quickly as I could.

That day and the next, Alan was a mass of convulsions. Nothing could settle him and I didn't know what to do. My nine-month-old baby was being taken over by these terrible attacks of shaking and shrieking and going into spasms. I phoned Dr

O'Doherty but couldn't reach him. Another doctor came out instead, and this doctor said he could find nothing wrong with Alan. I managed to get through to Dr O'Doherty at his clinic in Temple Street Hospital to tell him about Alan's condition. The doctor was annoyed with me for bothering him so much. I had to wait until the next official appointment to see him again.

I had begun to learn—the hard way—not to trust people. Time and again I had been completely ignored by the medics. My days of being an obedient young working-class mother were over.

———

In the following weeks I was watching Alan become more and more ill. He was drifting away before my very eyes. When the second appointment with Dr O'Doherty came around, he was not at the clinic. There was a female doctor there instead, and I was unhappy with this because I had become so concerned about Alan and wanted to see the same doctor again. This other doctor wanted me to strip Alan off and lie him on an examination bed. This had a sheet of disposable paper on it that was stained and I told her I would only lie Alan on a fresh sheet of paper. This annoyed her. She put down fresh paper from a roll and then gave Alan what I thought was a very basic examination. She said that Alan was well nourished and well cared for. She had no opinion on what the problem with him might be, however, and said I should book a new appointment with Dr O'Doherty.

A few weeks later I had my new appointment with Dr O'Doherty, who gave Alan an intensive check-over. He asked if Alan had received his third vaccination injection and I told him he had. When the doctor sat Alan on the desk, Alan fell over—not even putting his hand out to stop himself. As I watched all this I was wondering to myself what the doctor was looking for. He was now seeing all the things I knew had been lost from Alan. Dr

O'Doherty said he thought Alan needed more exercise and said he would arrange for him to be seen by a Dr Barry at the Central Remedial Clinic. He also said he would arrange for a lumbar-puncture test and told me to bring Alan to the clinic at Temple Street Children's Hospital.

As he ended the examination, Dr O'Doherty asked a question that had nothing to do with Alan but which gave me the first real clue as to what was going on: he wanted to know what Kevin's profession was. Looking back, I'm sure that if I had said Kevin was in the medical or legal profession, the doctor would have collapsed with fright. I felt he asked the question because he was trying to figure out if we were the kind of people who could cause trouble. What was he afraid of?

I went home from that appointment and I started giving the whole thing some serious thought. That was the day I started to suspect the vaccinations. But then again I kept thinking, that's medicine. Alan's worsening condition and the fact that his spasms and convulsions coincided with the last two vaccinations did not to my mind seem linked. If no doctor said they were linked, who was I to suggest they were?

I kept thinking about Alan's early months. His birth had gone well. He had been tested for development from birth, shown to be in perfect health and he had been given the best of everything. I was so fussy with my kids that I wouldn't even buy them tinned foods because I believed these were full of artificial ingredients and so I would buy the best vegetables and liquidise them. If Alan was healthy, happy and well fed, it didn't make sense that he could become so sick. The only thing different was those shots. Nothing else had disturbed him and, even though I had been told again and again that his reaction to the shots was nothing to worry about, they were the only possible source of Alan's sickness. I remembered the state Tracey had been in after her vaccinations— screaming with upset. She had recovered, although she needed treatment for her eyes. Alan had gone from normal development to this terrible state. There had to be a reason why a healthy child became so ill.

I decided to make a phone call. I rang the Department of Health and asked whom I could speak to about vaccinations. I was put through to Brendan O'Donnell who was Chief Medical Officer. I told him that my son had reached the age where he was due for his vaccinations and I had read somewhere that the whooping cough vaccine could, in some cases, cause brain damage. I said I was concerned about having my child vaccinated.

"Well we've heard these reports all right," he said, "but if we're talking statistics then I would say one in a million. So I'd say you'd be very foolish not to have it done."

"But is it possible this damage can happen," I asked.

"It seems to be," he replied, "though the statistics and chances are so remote you are far better off vaccinating the child. The diseases are so dangerous and the risk is so remote."

"One in a million?"

"If it's even one in a million," he said. "But the damage is possible."

"You're talking to the mother of one in a million," I said, "because I've been trying to find out what destroyed my son and I've been getting absolutely nowhere, until now."

He started shouting down the phone at me, saying this was the most underhanded trick anyone could pull and how dare I use him in that way.

"Well, I'll put it to you another way," I replied. "If I were to ring you up and say, 'I think my son has massive brain damage because of his pertussis vaccine', would you agree with me?"

"Of course I wouldn't," he said.

"Then how else was I to find out? All I wanted to know was if it was possible. At least now I know it is."

He slammed down the phone.

I told Kevin what had happened that day. "The vaccinations did this to Alan and these people are going to cover it up," I said.

I didn't have a shred of proof, but I knew inside that I was right.

————

Alan was no longer the healthy and growing child I had brought into the world. I had become aware of this, and then others started to see it. I would be wheeling him in his pram out shopping and women might come up to look in at him and ask his name. "He's gorgeous," they'd say. They'd be googling at him and he wouldn't respond and they wouldn't know what to say to me. People would be shocked. He looked so lovely, but he was so remote. There was no visible sign that people noticed about Alan. He just didn't react to them, or to me.

I decided to test Alan's hearing. Dr O'Doherty had suggested that this could be the cause of Alan's remoteness. We were in the kitchen and I told Kevin to watch Alan, who was sitting with his back to me in his baby chair. I opened the back door and smashed a milk bottle against the wall. Alan was startled by the noise. It wasn't a very scientific way of testing him, but it showed that he could hear. We were referred to an audiologist at Temple Street Children's Hospital, a Sister Mary Lydia, who tested Alan's hearing and was of the opinion that if he had a hearing problem, it was "very slight indeed".

One night Alan had a very serious convulsion. We wrapped him in a blanket, got in the car and rushed him to Crumlin Hospital. He was rigid, grey, screeching. They gave him some medicine and sent us home. No more was made of it. The medics were either ignorant of what the symptoms could mean, or they knew what had happened to Alan and that his case was hopeless.

When I brought Alan to Dr Barry at the CRC, I was told that Alan was physically all right but a bit slow. He gave me a set of exercises for him and said there was no reason why my son wouldn't be walking perfectly in due course. It was the start of twice-weekly visits to the CRC with Alan for these remedial exercises.

Kevin and I went to see Dr O'Doherty at his Temple Street clinic. He told us the lumbar puncture was clear, and then arranged for an EEG test to be carried out in Crumlin Children's Hospital. He still would not tell us what he thought could be wrong with Alan. In fact, he thought we were over-anxious parents. When Alan was referred for an EEG in April 1974, the results of the test came back saying that although Alan was a 'very restless, crying baby' there were no abnormalities. This was a result that baffled me. By that time Alan was having several convulsions every day.

In the months after Alan's last vaccination, as I kept going to these different doctors, I always had the sense they were holding something back from me. "He was all right when he was born," I would tell them, "so why is he like this now? Why is he not responding to us? Why does he not laugh any more? Why does he not sit up any more?"

There was never a clear answer. In all that time I never once heard a doctor give a diagnosis of what was wrong with Alan. No one said Alan is autistic, epileptic, or whatever. The most any doctor would say was that he had a problem. One thing I was told was that if a child is going to have any form of infantile spasm, it would happen at that age. Which itself begs the question—why vaccinate babies at an age when they are at risk of such things? But as I learned, infantile spasms normally pass. With Alan, the spasms had become convulsions and he was on anti-convulsive medication that wasn't working.

I wanted to get an appointment to see Dr O'Doherty again. I was frantic to find out what was happening with our son, but the nearest appointment was weeks away. I asked if I would be able to see him sooner if I arranged to do so privately—outside the free medical health system. I was told I could.

I got sick of this doctor—I could never get answers from him—and went to my GP, Dr Frank Dwane, asking him to recommend us to another paediatrician. Dr Dwane suggested instead that I should bring Alan to a neurologist. At that time I didn't even know what a neurologist was. I arranged an appointment to see Niall O'Donohoe, the man who had carried out Alan's EEG test at Crumlin Hospital. By doing this I was going over Dr O'Doherty's head as far as medical practice was concerned. Usually it was the GP who referred a patient to a specialist.

Our appointment with Dr O'Donohoe at Our Lady's Hospital for Sick Children in Crumlin came around. Kevin and I went in with Alan. We had decided in advance what our approach would be. Previously, any time we had questioned the vaccine, the medical people didn't want to know. So we decided we would go into Dr O'Donohoe and play ignorant.

"This is my son," I told Niall O'Donohoe. "He was a lovely happy little child, and now he's like this. Can someone tell me what's wrong with him?"

After the examination, O'Donohoe told us that Alan was mildly mentally retarded. I told him again how healthy Alan had been in his early months and about the symptoms that had developed since then.

Before we left that appointment Dr O'Donohoe made an arrangement to meet Kevin and me with Dr O'Doherty at Temple Street Hospital. He was concerned that we had broken protocol by not approaching him through Dr O'Doherty. It was something I saw often down the years—medical people more concerned for each other than for their patients.

When we went to that appointment, as Kevin and I were sitting in the waiting room with Alan in a buggy, I looked out and I saw the two doctors outside together. They were waving their hands and shaking their heads. It was obvious to me they were having some kind of argument. Though I couldn't hear a word, I felt sure they were arguing about Alan and I would love to have known what they were saying. When they met us, they announced that Alan needed to become a patient at St Michael's House.

"What is St Michael's?" I asked.

"It's a hospital for the handicapped."

We were given an appointment to see Dr Barbara Stokes there. "Alan's future lies there," we were told. When we brought Alan to Dr Stokes, I told her directly what we believed had caused this damage to Alan.

"Did you come here by train, a car, or a taxi," she asked.

"Why?"

"Well you could have been killed on your way here, or you could have stayed at home. You took a chance and lost."

"Do you think this is what happened to Alan?" I asked.

"More than likely," she said. "That's probably why we have so many people in institutions but don't know what happened to them."

It was the only time anyone in the medical profession in Ireland had ever said directly to us that the vaccine caused the damage to Alan. Although Dr Stokes never denied saying this to me, she also said I would never be able to prove that the vaccine had destroyed Alan. "In my lifetime," she said, "it will never be written on hospital paper that this could happen to anyone receiving a vaccine." It was as if doctors had been told never to state on paper their knowledge of damage being caused by vaccines. Later I would seize one opportunity when a doctor accidentally broke that rule.

Dr Corry, who had delivered Alan, said the same thing. In those days doctors did not break rank on support for the National Vaccination Programme. I think they were afraid of the truth. And yet, unbeknownst to people like me, it was something they discussed openly among themselves.

In September 1974 in Dublin, at a time when I was trying to find out what was happening to my son, there was a newspaper report of a discussion on 'Problems and Progress of Childhood Immunisation' as part of Medical Postgraduate Week. The event was organised by the Irish Medical Association and Wellcome

Ireland Ltd (the manufacturers of the vaccine). *The Irish Times* reported that, at this conference, the main speaker was Dr Freestone of the Department of Clinical Immunology in the Wellcome Research Laboratories in England. This doctor suggested that there should be some machinery created whereby the victims of serious side effects from pertussis or other vaccinations should be able to receive compensation. To quote the article, Dr Freestone acknowledged that brain damage did occur, even if the incidence was rare, and that the pertussis vaccine should never be given 'to a child who had a medical history of convulsions, to a child who was seriously ill, nor should a second dose be given to a child who had a severe (if not necessarily serious) reaction to the first'.

It seemed that experts knew things—and talked openly about such things—that the doctors in health clinics hadn't been told about. Or that paediatrician Dr O'Doherty hadn't heard about—things they would deny when the public realised the danger. Not everyone was ignorant of the facts. After Alan was destroyed, the district nurse who came to us said of the vaccine: 'I wouldn't give it to my dog.'

——

One day, Kevin and I did something very simple. We walked into a chemist and asked the pharmacist if there were books that would give information about the risks of vaccines. He said there was indeed a journal that gave full information about all drugs, including their side effects, but that this journal was not for lay people. We told the man what was happening to us and our worries about Alan. He was very sweet and very supportive.

"I can't give you the journal," he said. Then he showed me exactly where the journal was and said, "Now I'm going to have a chat with your husband about the weather and I'm going to turn my back on you so I won't know if you take it."

Kevin and I went home with the journal, the official publication of the Council of the Pharmaceutical Society of Great Britain, published in 1947. Concerning the vaccine it stated:

> though rare, encephalopathies have been noted in association with inoculations of vaccine; American workers now recommend that no child should be injected with large doses of pertussis vaccine if there is a family or personal history of convulsions or if the child has any form of illness pertaining in any way to the central nervous system.

I have a family history of epilepsy. I was seeing here, for the first time, that because of this Alan should not have been given the whooping cough part of the three-in-one. Why had no one in the medical profession asked me or warned me? Why had, so far, only one of the doctors dealing with Alan told me that this was the likely cause?

By the time Dr O'Donohoe did a second EEG in October 1974, his conclusions about Alan had changed drastically. 'The record shows a marked deterioration since the previous tracing', his report began, and it concluded by stating: 'The record shows very frequent generalised epileptic disturbances.' Alan's diagnosis changed from being 'mildly' handicapped to 'moderately' handicapped.

I had a further appointment to see Dr Stokes, but when I arrived she wasn't there. By this time I was losing any notion that people in the medical profession should be treated with some kind of reverence. I sat in the office and refused to leave until I had a new appointment. The secretary phoned Dr Stokes, who arranged to meet me the following day. At that meeting Dr Stokes informed me that Alan was an epileptic who would need daily medication for the rest of his life. She said also that Alan had fallen into the 'severely mentally retarded' class. She prescribed medication for his condition—medication that I would not have received for my son for another six weeks if I had done the secretary's bidding and obediently gone away.

Kevin wanted us to go for a holiday. Our lives had become one long struggle to find out what was happening with Alan. Kevin enquired about finding a place where Alan would be looked after while we went away for a break. He was told there was one hospital that would take Alan in, and so Kevin went there to see if the place was suitable. What he saw, I never saw. But he told me he was brought into a place for severely disabled and handicapped children. He saw things he had never imagined—some terrible cases—and our Alan was being looked upon as one of these. Kevin walked out of the hospital and cried bitter tears. We found a different place for Alan to stay while we took our short break.

———

Alan's condition became far worse. He was having up to eight convulsions a day. Time and again we would have to rush him into hospital. One time when Alan had been extremely ill we brought him yet again to Crumlin Hospital. Because of his convulsions, he was kept in the room next to the nurses' offices so they could see him at all times through the glass. Kevin and I were in the room with Alan when I saw the nurse leave Alan's file on a cabinet in the office. I saw my chance to find out what was going on.

"You keep nix," I told Kevin. "I'll slip in and get it."

Kevin stood out in the corridor—ready to make a noise if anyone came along—as I went into the office. I got the file and hid it in a shopping bag I had. I then went off to lock myself in a toilet to read the file.

"You won't understand the reports," Kevin told me. "So just read the conclusions."

We were like two spies trying to find the truth we had a right to know. I went into a toilet cubicle and opened the file. A letter immediately caught my eye. It was between two doctors involved in the case but who cannot be named for legal reasons as I have no proof of seeing the letter. It said: 'This boy has been destroyed by pertussis vaccine. Both parents are very intelligent. Please advise', or words to that effect.

Afraid of being caught, I put the file back in the office. If only I had that chance again, I would have kept that file. Kevin and I had an appointment with Dr Stokes a few weeks later and I told her I had read the letter. She was angry with us for having read private correspondence. Kevin is a gentle man, but he got up and went around the desk to her.

"Kevin, don't touch her," I shouted, and he kept control.

"One way or the other," he said, "we'll find out the truth."

But stealing that file and hiding in a toilet was how I found out the true medical opinion on Alan. I knew then that the vaccine had destroyed my son and that the medical profession was determined to deny the fact. They wanted to protect themselves and the national immunisation programme. It was then that I decided to go public. If Alan had been damaged, then I wanted to know if there were more children like him. The only way to do that was to go to the newspapers with our story.

My eyes were about to be opened. My search for the truth about my son would turn into a decades-long battle with the Irish government and the health system.

Chapter 3

THE ASSOCIATION FOR VACCINE-DAMAGED CHILDREN

Chief Medical Officer Brendan O'Donnell had told me on the phone that brain damage from the vaccine happened to one in a million. But could it happen more often than that? I phoned all the newspapers in Ireland explaining my situation and telling them about that phone call. I saw it as my way to find out what was going on. The *Sunday Press* decided to do a feature on Alan, sending the reporter Ginnie Kinnealy and a photographer out to us. The article, published on 2 March 1975, was the first time our story was told to people in Ireland. We had no idea what kind of response might ensue.

When we got the paper that Sunday morning, there was our story with a photograph of us with Alan and the heading 'The tragedy of one child in 50,000', which was the figure the reporter's research had come up with. The report included this comment (imagine how Kevin and I felt about it) from the deputy Chief Medical Officer in the Department of Health: 'Remember that whooping cough is traditionally a prevalent disease in this country which has claimed many babies' lives and has left others crippled with bronchial troubles. Their numbers are far higher than those of children who become brain-damaged through misapplied injections. So unless there are definite contra-indications all babies should have the full 3 in 1 injections.' It was a plain admission and a shrugging-off of what had happened to our son.

Kevin and I wondered if anyone else in the country would write to the paper with a similar story. We'd have to wait and see what the coming week would bring. Maybe the reporter would contact us with news of another case like Alan's. Then there was a ring at the door. A man stood there with the newspaper in his hand. He had driven up from the country that morning when he read the article. He said he believed his son had been damaged this way and that his child's story was the same as Alan's.

That was only the beginning. Letters did indeed start coming in to the offices of the *Sunday Press*. We started finding terrible stories of sadness, and there was a huge reaction around the country. I was starting to find my answer: I wasn't alone.

By the following Sunday the paper was reporting the response. We had received letters from over a dozen people with stories like ours. I was reading all these letters, and time and again I was seeing the same thing that had happened to Alan. It was always the same reaction to the vaccine: spasms and fits and perfect children left damaged. And always the same denial by the doctors, who said it was colic or whatever and just went on jabbing needles into the children until the children were destroyed. Then the families, just like Kevin and me, were left to bounce around from one medical expert to another who would shrug their shoulders and offer no explanation. Something had been happening in the country but no one had yet raised the alarm. The doctors in these cases had either kept hush about them or were working in such ignorance that they knew nothing about the dangers and the destruction. When we put all the stories together, there was such a clear pattern that we knew we were sharing the same battle.

That same weekend, Dr Stokes had taken Alan in to St Ultan's Hospital for a full assessment. She had contacted Kevin during the week, expressing her wish to do so, and we were very pleased that Alan was getting this swift attention. It took us decades, and the release of documents under the Freedom of Information Act, to learn that this offer was prompted by the wish to give a full medical assessment of Alan for a report being prepared for the Tánaiste.

Kevin and I told the *Sunday Press* that we were going to set up a group—the Irish Association for Vaccine-Damaged Children. We had two aims: that not another child would ever be damaged by the vaccine; and that proper care and compensation would be given to those already damaged. Above all, I knew that Alan was not the only one. I felt then that I had to fight on behalf of my son. If his life had been ruined because of these vaccinations, I would see to it that the sacrifice of his life was made to save others. That was the least I could do for him.

In England, meanwhile, the Labour MP Jack Ashley was championing the cause of Rosemary Fox, an Irish woman married and living there. Rosemary's daughter, Helen, had been brain-damaged by the polio vaccine and Rosemary had set up an Association for Vaccine-Damaged Children. The Association brought 281 cases of vaccine damage to light in Great Britain. As more than half these cases were blamed on the whooping cough vaccine, Rosemary focused her work on that. She was able to access all the medical literature showing the known risks of vaccines, risks that the public were not being informed about. She was able to show that other countries, Germany for instance, already had a system of compensating and supporting vaccine-damaged children.

By early 1975, thanks to Rosemary's determination, pressure was building on the British government to help and compensate the parents of these children. There was talk of a commission of inquiry and it was being compared with the Thalidomide tragedy. Articles were appearing in British newspapers, and when I read them I contacted Rosemary. When we talked on the phone, I decided I would go to England and meet her.

Rosemary lives in a small village called Shipton-on-Stour. I had all kinds of directions for train connections, and I was loaded down with files and research I wanted to show her. I had never travelled abroad alone before, and my heart was jumping out of my chest when I finally arrived at this little train station, hoping she would be there or else I would be lost in the middle of nowhere. I didn't know what Rosemary looked like, but I had told her in advance the colour of the coat I would be wearing. When I got off the train and was looking up and down the platform, this woman walked towards me, smiling.

"You're Vera, aren't you?" she said.

I grabbed her like she was my sister. "Thank God you're here," I said.

I stayed with her for three days. Rosemary is a lovely and kind woman. She was living in a beautiful old farmhouse and there I met her daughter Helen, who was severely brain-damaged. Helen was already a teenager by then and Rosemary was wonderful with her. I remember comparing my little baby Alan to Helen and trying to imagine what it would be like to be caring for him at that age.

Rosemary and I would sit up for hours talking and the trip was a huge education for me. I learned about what I was really up against. During those three days she introduced me to Jack Ashley MP and put me in contact with a man who I think educated me more than anyone else, Prof. Gordon Stewart of Glasgow University's Department of Community Medicine.

I came back from Rosemary Fox a different woman. I had a lot more information and a lot less naivety. Two delusions I had been raised with—that you must trust doctors and believe the government—had collapsed. Over those days in England I was advised on the best strategies for bringing out the truth. And I learned my first sense of what might lie ahead for me and for parents in my situation. I would never have expected this in my life, but I was about to become the leading voice in what would be a major Irish controversy.

Gordon Stewart was in Dublin for a conference not long after that trip, and he contacted me. When he met me he was both delighted and angry. "Oh my God," he said, "so it's going on in Ireland, too. You have no idea of the battle that's ahead of you."

The extraordinary thing about Gordon is that he was one of the researchers who had worked on the initial trials in the 1940s preparing the vaccine in Britain. He had known of its side effects—he had even referred to it as a 'witch's brew' of toxins—but had believed its benefits outweighed its dangers. I had always believed that if it's medicine it must be good for you. When I brought Alan to the Edenmore Health Clinic for his vaccinations—the first, the second and the third—I was placing my trust in a profession and a government that I was sure existed for the good of all. I didn't question what they were jabbing into my baby. I was learning from Gordon, too late, that people like me and Alan didn't matter when compared with the welfare of 'the herd'. Every vaccine introduces a small amount of the disease it is to prevent into the body: with the pertussis vaccine that meant injecting whole dead pertussis bacteria into the baby. I didn't know that even at the time of Alan's vaccinations there were already new versions of the vaccine being produced that did not inject the whole bacteria but only those parts thought necessary to trigger immunity. That new vaccine, however, was considered too expensive for national vaccination programmes.

Over the decades following the launch of the pertussis vaccine, Gordon Stewart saw that a third of those vaccinated still got whooping cough, and he came to the conclusion that the vaccine was too dangerous. He described it as "intrinsically bad for all children and very dangerous for some", saying it was given at a very sensitive time in a baby's life for infantile convulsions and cot deaths. He had been speaking out for years against the dangers of government policies of mass immunisation, and he became a member of the British Committee on the Safety of Medicines.

"The truth is known," he said, "but the doctors aren't going to do anything about it, scientists can't do anything about it, and the politicians won't do anything about it because the common good is at stake. It will take people like you and Rosemary to scream from high heaven 'you destroyed my child'." Gordon believed there were hundreds in institutions and hospitals who were the undiagnosed victims of vaccine damage. He told me something that upset me very much.

"The children of people like you and Rosemary—children who are well nourished and well cared for—don't need vaccination," he said. "It's needed to protect undernourished and unhealthy children in crowded, underprivileged areas." Children in such poverty and hardship stood far less chance of surviving these diseases and were also far more likely to contract them. But no government and no social scheme would admit that and so 'the herd'—the whole community—was immunised.

"They don't want to admit this is happening," he warned me. He knew what they were capable of and I didn't. I believed back then that politicians and medics had integrity.

"If they see that these children have been destroyed, they're going to do something," I said.

"They'll bury them first," was his reply.

———

The reaction to the vaccine revelations in England was a far cry from the reaction in Ireland. English doctors never denied the dangers of the vaccine, and there was little Rosemary needed to do once she had succeeded in discovering the truth and bringing the clear facts of this terrible problem to the attention of politicians and the public. In Ireland, however, it seemed there was a wish to keep people in ignorance and so there was a much bigger gap to be bridged. When Rosemary Fox launched her campaign, she was praised for her commitment to the truth. In

Ireland, I came to be seen as a damn nuisance.

As soon as the story about Alan and children like him made headlines, the Irish Medical Association started warning of the dangers of an epidemic of whooping cough if people stopped bringing their babies for vaccination. But they also said that all parents should first bring their babies to their family doctor to check if their child was suitable for the vaccine. This was news to me and any other parent who had obediently brought their children to medical centres throughout the country. As I wrote in a letter to the newspaper at the time, it showed that the IMA did not trust the health clinics to take such precautions themselves. A war of words was starting between the medical profession and the public they were supposed to be caring for. I was learning that the medical profession looked first at how to stop anyone questioning their wisdom. The problem itself took second place.

We held the first meeting of the Association in our house in Coolock on 22 March 1975. By then, even more cases had come to light. John O'Connell TD, who was also a doctor, attended the meeting. He and others had asked questions in the Dáil about the whooping cough vaccine. The Tánaiste and Minister for Health, Brendan Corish, was trying to put everyone's mind at rest while not really knowing what to do. The *Sunday Press*, in an open letter to Corish, pointed out that five European countries, plus Japan, had already set up compensation schemes for the victims of the whooping cough vaccine—Germany had set up its scheme in 1962. The newspaper also complained about the way the government was trying to avoid admitting there was a problem.

We were soon invited to meet Brendan Corish. We met him in May for the first time and my hopes were high that the truth would be acknowledged and action taken. As I was soon to learn, the only thing he and politicians generally cared about was making the problem go away.

The Association very quickly became a loud voice in Ireland. People had sympathy for babies damaged by vaccine, and people were worried about the risks they were taking with their own babies. Loud voices are heard by politicians, and the local Fianna Fáil TD in Coolock was quick to offer his support. That was Charlie Haughey. Haughey phoned me and offered me his secretarial services.

"The work you are doing is wonderful," he told me, "but you're only a housewife and you're trying to mind your children. I have offices out here in Kinsealy and my secretary can help you. Any typing or photocopying or anything else you need, just come out." He gave me the code for opening the security gate.

I told Kevin and he started laughing. "I think he fancies you," he said.

"The dirty old feck," I said.

"You're not going out there, are you?"

"No I'm not. I'll do it myself."

Charlie often phoned to see how things were progressing, and was always a great ally in the campaign.

While back in September, Wellcome had, in Dublin, openly discussed the risks involved in vaccines with members of the Irish Medical Association, things changed when the Association for Vaccine-Damaged Children was launched. Prof. Irene Hillary, then of the University College Dublin Department of Microbiology, is a woman I would cross paths with many times over the coming decades. She gave a speech addressing the Irish Society of Medical Officers and was quoted in a newspaper report as warning that if children were not immunised against whooping cough there would be an epidemic. She noted that there had already been a rise in the incidence of whooping cough and that "the upsurge in figures might grow more alarming for this year and next year". The *Evening Herald* article stated: 'Dr Hillary said children not immunised were at much greater risk of suffering brain damage. And she feared that the recent controversy over pertussis—whooping cough—had caused such alarm that mothers were deciding against immunisation of their children without medical advice.' No one had told me there was *any* risk of brain damage, yet here she was saying that those not immunised were at 'greater' risk than those immunised.

––––

In June, I took Alan to Lourdes. I was never big into prayers or religion, but I knew that people were cured there and I would do anything to have Alan cured. My view was that God didn't want Alan to be brain-damaged. After all, Alan wasn't born that way, so maybe if I brought him to Lourdes, God would cure him.

My main impression of Lourdes is that it's a terribly sad place. Kevin and I decided that we would take part in all the various prayers and processions. I wanted to be sure I did everything for fear of missing out on a miracle happening for Alan. There was an event called the 'Blessing of the Sick', where all the sick gather around. They always put the children at the front, so we were there with Alan. Behind us were people in wheelchairs and behind them again the people who could stand. It was shocking and heartbreaking to see so much suffering. The priests went around blessing everyone individually. I noticed that people held their hands out, palms facing up, and I did the same. I wasn't going to miss out on doing anything to get God's attention for Alan.

Kevin couldn't bring Alan into the baths, I think partly because he didn't believe in Lourdes. I was put in a sack-like dress and got into the water and then Alan, in just his nappy, was lowered down to me. The people working there just wanted me to dip Alan in the water, but I believed that unless that water covered his head, his brain couldn't be cured. I dipped Alan's head into the cold water and he cried. Then, carrying Alan, I walked to the end of the bath and kissed the feet of the statue of Our Lady. I did it each day we were there. Always, Kevin would be there looking on and waiting for me. He'd put his arm around me and say, "Come on and we'll get a cup of coffee."

I remember one day sitting in the huge basilica, with Alan in his buggy beside me, during a Mass with dozens of priests going around blessing the sick. All the prayers and ceremonies were huge events, yet there was always a mood of sadness in the place. I suppose everyone there had reached the last place of hope, beyond the bounds of what medicine could do. Behind all the prayer and ceremony was desperation.

Kevin and I would bring Alan in the buggy and we would sit for hours in front of the statue of Our Lady at the grotto. I said to Kevin that I was afraid there were too many people around and so maybe God couldn't concentrate on Alan. So I started waking Kevin up in the middle of the night so we could bring Alan to the statue while no one else was around. I prayed and prayed to Our Lady and to God to cure Alan. "Don't leave him like this," I begged them.

At that time I still had no idea how seriously damaged Alan was. At that young age, the gap between what Alan was capable of doing and what any child his age was capable of was not so extreme.

There was no miracle for Alan.

Three years later I would go back to Lourdes with Alan again when it was becoming clear to us just how severely handicapped he was. That time around, I took Lourdes much more seriously because Alan really needed help. I went that time with the realisation that I had lost my son and that he was destined to a life of suffering and only a miracle could bring him back. That was the first time I really experienced the desperation that everyone else felt. I prayed and begged all the harder. I pleaded with God and Our Lady to save my son. Again, there was no cure.

After that, I swore I'd never go back to Lourdes. I couldn't know then that I would have two more reasons in my life for going there.

When people contacted me with their stories about their children, the first thing I would tell them to do was to get the child's immunisation card—which showed the lot number and batch number for the vaccinations given. I would refer them to Dr Steevens' Hospital, where all such records were kept. More often than not, they would be told that something had happened and the records no longer existed—be it due to a flood, or a fire, or some misplacement. The only people who had such a record were people like me who had kept the cards from the time of the immunisations.

We held our first open public meeting at the North Star Hotel in Dublin. At the meeting people were telling the same story over and over again. Kevin and I and other parents were at the table along with a representative from the Department of Health— P.W. Flanagan. I had made up a form for people to fill out, giving the history of their stories, so that we could build up files of the cases we had found. We wanted to be an organised and effective voice for our children.

After that meeting, a woman came up to me. She was Angela Convey from Enfield, Co. Kildare. Her little daughter had died. She handed me a letter.

"I think I'll never get this to you," she said.

"What is it?"

"Prof. Conor Ward wrote to me after my daughter died. He says she got encephalitis from the pertussis vaccine and there was no known cure."

I read the letter, written in October 1971. There it was in black and white—a doctor in Ireland saying that the pertussis vaccine had caused brain damage. He wrote:

It would be unnatural if you did not feel greatly distressed by the fact that the injections which were necessary for your baby's protection against whooping cough and other diseases in fact caused a progressive condition from which recovery was not likely. Once we had observed the deterioration in Angela's capacity for interest and activity following her admission to hospital it was inevitable from the medical point of view that she would be permanently affected to some extent. The only treatment for her condition is ACTH and it is an unfortunate side-effect that patient's resistance is lowered and they cannot stand up to the stress of infection while on the treatment.

I was finally holding in my hand the proof I had hoped to find. Not only that, Ward was saying something that a doctor had once said to me about Alan but when I asked him to state so formally, he denied saying it: "It's a pity they didn't try ACTH." I later learned that if someone has a severe reaction to a medication, ACTH is used to counteract the effect. It only works if given as soon as possible after the reaction.

"How did you react when you got this letter?" I asked her.

"Well, at least I knew what killed her," she answered.

The woman had none of the anger I felt for the medical profession and was willing to accept what had happened. It was not until she heard about me that she decided she would give me the letter.

"Do you trust me?" I asked her.

"Yes," she said. "I don't care what happens now."

Angela's husband, John, had sent Ward's letter to Dr Brendan O'Donnell, who was Kildare County Medical Officer at the time of the child's death. O'Donnell, who had become the 'one-in-a-million' Chief Medical Officer when I contacted him, wrote back saying: 'I would point out that it would serve no purpose for you to report Angela's case to the Eastern Health Board because Our Lady's Hospital, Crumlin, is an independent voluntary hospital and the Eastern Health Board has no direct control over it.'

I could have immediately gone to the papers with the Convey letter. I could have made this the headline news of this first public meeting of the Association. Instead, I kept the letter a secret. I knew I should wait until the time was right.

In the end, we had 38 documented cases from around the country of children brain-damaged or killed by the vaccine. Of all the cases, only three were girls. This is a trend that I later discovered was common throughout the world. We gave the report to Brendan Corish in August 1975, expecting by then to have some tribunal or commission set up to deal with the problem. I had the feeling that we would be listened to, and all the early indications in newspaper reports were that the Department of Health and the Minister were aware of the problem.

In February 1976, we got his response. The Minister said:

1. The conditions to which the reports relate can be the result of one or more of a number of different causes. 2. The information furnished in the reports does not establish that the condition of any of the children was the outcome of the vaccine.

He wrote also that he saw no reason to 'make special provisions for the children concerned over and above that normally available to persons with similar afflictions'.

Corish probably hoped that was the end of the matter. It definitely was not.

In March 1976, Kevin and I brought Alan to Dr John Wilson, Consultant Neurologist at the Hospital for Sick Children at Ormond Street in London. Wilson had been one of the first doctors to state there was a link between the whooping cough vaccine and brain damage, and he had been interviewed on television and in the newspapers. He had done a great deal to help Rosemary Fox in her work. He examined Alan and he asked me several questions. His opinion was:

> Alan is severely mentally handicapped and suffers from myoclonic epilepsy. He may have suffered from infantile spasms as well as major fits in the past. The circumstantial evidence suggesting that his condition results from encephalopathic complications of DPT vaccine, of which the pertussis component is strongly suspect, is strong.

After all the times I had been to doctors and specialists with my son, Wilson was the first medical person to directly express that view about Alan. I had to go to England to meet someone who could put down in black and white the possibility that Alan had been damaged by the vaccine. In Ireland, I'd had to steal a file and hide in a toilet to find out the medical opinion on Alan. No wonder I became more and more disillusioned with Ireland over the years of my battle.

By that time Kevin and I had also gone to a solicitor to start the process of putting a court case together against the Eastern Health Board. This was a huge task—taking on a government organisation. We felt it was the right way to bring this injustice to light. Unfortunately, the company we chose had no experience of dealing with such matters and that attempt ultimately led us nowhere.

———

I was always afraid that Alan wouldn't get the care other children in his situation would get. My going public had changed the way I was treated by the medical profession. Their first priority from then on was to wash their hands of me and Alan as best they could. If he was in hospital, the hospital couldn't wait to discharge him. Every time something went into the press it was worse. Because of his condition, there were often emergencies, but when we arrived at a hospital with him it was more a matter of putting up defences than of showing concern for Alan. Word would be passed around the hospital staff that I was there: the woman who had gone to the newspapers with the story about her vaccine-damaged child.

Once, the Minister for Health insisted that Alan be taken into Crumlin Hospital for examination to see if the vaccine could be the cause of his condition. When Kevin and I would go in to see Alan, there was never a time when one doctor would talk with us alone to answer our queries. Always other doctors would be called in to witness the conversation. For me and Kevin this became funny—wondering how many they would bring in next time we asked a question. We were seen as trouble-makers who had made accusations against the medical profession and the State.

Even my name meant trouble. When parents came to me in the Association, I would ask them what the doctors were saying about their child. I would tell them not to believe the doctors and then give them other questions to ask. People were going back to Niall O'Donohoe saying, "Vera Duffy told us . . ." and they came back to tell me he would say he didn't want to hear my name mentioned in his office. As far as he was concerned, I was someone who knew nothing about medicine and I was undermining him.

The medical profession in Ireland had been dealing with disabled children and in my opinion they had been quietly picking up the pieces of vaccine damage until I came along and started asking for answers. What made me dangerous was that I questioned their authority. People were coming to me with stories identical to what had happened with Alan, and I was telling them what I had learned and what had not been explained by the medical profession. I was encouraging them to think again about what they had been told. If the child was well, why has it become brain-damaged? If medical records show no cause for handicap, then why does a healthy child become handicapped? These parents then went back to the doctors and specialists armed with some knowledge, and that made me out to be someone interfering where I had no right. I later got my hands on a letter about me from one medic to another saying, "This woman is extremely intelligent, which is very worrying."

Some parents backed off from me and the Association, afraid that their children would not get proper treatment if the doctors were annoyed with them. As for me, I only wished that someone before me had gone public so that I might have understood the dangers of vaccination. If that had happened, my Alan would have been safe. But it didn't happen that way. Alan was the victim whose case lifted the lid on it all. When I came along, the damage had already been happening for decades. It wasn't just Alan as an infant and more infants after him. There were teenagers and young adults whose parents had the same story to tell. It was a backlog of tragedies, and I was bringing the whole sad story to the surface, though I think I only picked up the crumbs of what was really going on. I imagine that in the 40s and 50s brain-damaged children were put into mental institutions and the cause of their condition was never questioned. The very fact that I was asking questions should have been a good thing. I was raising awareness and raising the concerns of parents. But that was not the Irish culture of the time. We mothers were there to breed, pray, obey and shut up. It was like that time when I was put in psychiatric care because of postnatal depression: if you raised a problem then you *became* the problem.

———

In England, meanwhile, Jack Ashley and Rosemary Fox were making progress. While the Association kept writing to the politicians here in Ireland, over in England in 1977 it was finally accepted that children had been damaged by vaccines and compensation should be given. The National Childhood

Encephalopathy Study was launched—an attempt to set exact figures for the risk involved in the pertussis vaccine. A turning point was when Prof. Gordon Stewart wrote to Health Secretary David Ennals warning of the dangers of the pertussis vaccine. 'I have complained to the Department,' he wrote, 'that whooping cough vaccine is not effective and that the risk of brain damage is therefore unacceptably high.' The British Ombudsman then also asked that individual cases be sent to him, and I sent him four sample cases from Ireland. He could not deal with our cases, but he later said that the British health authorities had been negligent in not warning parents of the dangers of the whooping cough vaccine.

At this stage doctors and politicians in the UK were throwing figures back and forth, and the conclusion being presented was that the risks from whooping cough were statistically higher than the risks from the whooping cough vaccine. They were saying: 'It's better that a few babies are destroyed by the vaccine than that more babies are destroyed by the disease.' No one at that time was denying the risk and the damage. All they couldn't agree on were the numbers involved: how many destroyed lives were the price of an effective vaccine programme.

The breakthrough in Britain brought another push from us. I was writing to all the politicians again, and the matter was raised once more in the Dáil. Brendan Corish agreed to meet us to try to resolve this issue that he'd hoped was over and done with. We had the meeting in Leinster House. By this time there had been a huge amount of publicity around me and the Association and the whole issue of vaccinating children. I had been calling for an inquiry, and this meeting was arranged for me to meet Minister for Health Corish and his henchmen, as I thought of them, to demand action. Dr John O'Connell TD was with me, and Prof. Gordon Stewart had flown over from Scotland to join me at the meeting. We met Charlie Haughey at Buswell's Hotel and we all went in to the meeting together. I felt at last that we parents would be heard and our concerns acted on.

At the meeting I listed the changes that were needed to make the vaccination process safer. They typically denied there could be any risk or danger attached to the vaccination process.

"We're the Department of Health. We would have information on it if there was such a risk," was their line. "You can't inject something into the bloodstream that then damages the brain. Nothing can break the blood-brain barrier." They went on and on, assuring me that they were the experts and would know if there was any danger. So I sat back and listened until they had talked themselves out. Then I took the Conor Ward letter out of my bag and slammed it down on the table.

"I will have that letter on the front page of every newspaper by this evening," I said, "unless you make these changes."

They read the letter and went pale.

"How dare you treat me like an idiot," I said. "Don't you ever again insult my intelligence."

"Please don't print this letter," I was asked. They totally changed their attitude. They realised I was not someone they could fob off.

"Now we're really talking," I said.

They agreed to have a panel of experts investigate the link between the vaccination programme and brain damage. Reporters were waiting outside, and I told them I was "very, very happy with the outcome of the meeting". I felt I had really achieved something.

In the space of a couple of years I had gone from being a working-class housewife knowing nothing about these medical dangers to being the founder of an organisation that was forcing the State to face up to this terrible problem. The health system was not going to ruin my son's life and then cover up the cause. I was still naive enough to believe I could win.

In May we were told that the expert panel would be set up and we were sent a list of names from which the panel would be drawn. We would be able to nominate our own representative on the panel, and we were to have a meeting with the Department of Health to discuss our choice.

But by then I was starting to have other things on my mind. A doctor had once advised me, "don't get bitter, Vera. Have another baby." And I did. The baby was very much planned, even though all through my pregnancy I was doing battle with the government and the medical profession and I was doing my best to care for Alan. I was constantly giving of myself. No matter how exhausted I might be, I would never refuse to accept a phone call or do whatever I could to help someone who came for advice from the Association. I was a one-woman show.

By the summer the politicians also had other things on their minds. There was a general election, and Fianna Fáil were pushing to get back into power after four years of the Coalition holding the majority.

In July 1977 our new baby was born. I was so much in the news that there was even a piece about the birth in the paper. I was asked if I would have more children and I answered, "loads more". We named our daughter Renee.

When Renee was born I felt that this would somehow help me to live again. She was absolutely gorgeous and I adored her. When I was at home with Renee, life was nice again. We had Tracey, Alan and Renee and we were enjoying family life. We were getting on with our lives after the tragedy of what had happened to Alan. Needless to say, I would never allow Renee to be vaccinated.

Fianna Fáil won the election, and the man who had been our great political ally when we were dealing with Brendan Corish became the new Minister for Health: Charlie Haughey. I was delighted with the news. He and I had always stayed in contact. Sometimes he would phone for a chat to see how I was getting along. I was looking forward to being able to deal with him now as the one person who could champion our cause. He contacted the Association, saying the expert group was ready to be presented with cases. When I heard this I was of course furious. We had been promised that the Association would be able to nominate a member of the expert panel. Haughey, now on the other side of the negotiating table, had conveniently forgotten that. A meeting of the Dublin members of the Association was immediately called and it was unanimously agreed that we would boycott the panel.

I was trying to carry it all towards some kind of justice. I wanted John Wilson on the panel. I wanted Prof. Gordon Stewart on the panel. These were not being accepted by the government for the simple reason that these were people who were on my side. My view was that unless the government included a medical adviser nominated by us, then the expert panel would not be fair and impartial and I therefore would not present them with Alan's case.

Meanwhile, in my battle for justice, I had made enemies in the medical profession. An example of this animosity came to the surface late in 1977. By that time Renee was four months old and Alan was being collected each morning to be brought to St Michael's House for his remedial treatment. But he was, of course, still having his fits. We had a call in the afternoon to say that Alan had been rushed to Crumlin Hospital, and in the early evening Kevin went up to see how Alan was. He was approached in the corridor by a female doctor who informed him that he must take Alan away with him. As Alan had been brought in that afternoon, Kevin pointed out that Alan should be kept in the hospital for at least 24 hours for observation. But the hospital insisted that Alan be taken away. The doctor said this was because of the controversy surrounding his case.

This time Kevin and I would not do what the medical profession asked. We had our allies and we had learned how to react to this kind of treatment. We called the newspapers to let them know the Children's Hospital was refusing to care for our sick child. We contacted Dr Wilson in London to let him know the situation and he offered to fly over and take care of Alan in the hospital. We contacted an agency to hire private nurses who would care for Alan. In other words, we stood up to the hospital and arranged our own medical care as a way of confronting them.

We soon found out what was happening. Niall O'Donohoe, the neurologist who had seen Alan in the past, did not want to treat him any more. He wrote to Barbara Stokes a letter that we later discovered:

> Your Registrar sent in Alan Duffy to this hospital yesterday under my care and without discussing the matter with me in the first place. For many reasons, some of which you know, I do not wish to have this child as my patient and I have recommended that he should be discharged back to Saint Michael's House. I am prepared to see him there in consultation with you, but that is as far as I am prepared to go.

The *Irish Independent* contacted the hospital for a comment on the story. I was then approached by Edward Tempany and I told him what to expect: that an English neurologist would come to treat Alan in the hospital, and that the English newspapers would soon be reporting on the story. I was also going to take out a writ preventing Niall O'Donohoe from treating anyone. If he wasn't going to treat Alan, then he wasn't going to carry on working. I was then told that O'Donohoe had left the country on holiday for three weeks.

I was brought to the boardroom of the hospital and lined up before me was the matron and several doctors. I sat before them and said, "All your heads will roll. You're putting a sick child out of your hospital." Kevin afterwards asked me not to make threats like that. But it seemed to me it was always a fight and there was no other option.

The hospital issued a statement saying, 'The consultant in charge made a clinical decision to have Alan Duffy discharged. The reason for his decision was in no way . . . because of the vaccine controversy.'

Alan was kept in the hospital for several days, during which time we had private nurses minding him 24 hours a day. By then I just didn't trust the hospital when I saw the way they could behave. It was the old story of taking the side of a medic rather than being on the side of a patient. I felt afraid that if Alan went into a convulsion there without me he could die.

When the time came to leave, the hospital would not let us pay the bill for the nurses we had hired. They obviously did not want us to show receipts of money we had paid for care they should have been giving. Tempany came to me and I picked up Alan and said, "He's an embarrassment to the medical profession. You don't know what to do with him." He gave no answer. What could he have said?

———

As that year drew to a close, there was an impasse between the Association and new Minister for Health Haughey. However, the matter of vaccine damage was about to reach the courts for the first time. In December the case of 4-year-old Daragh Murphy was heard in the High Court. His parents were suing both the doctor who had vaccinated their son, and the Eastern Health Board, for negligence. It was one of a few test cases which made its way to the court, and the battles of many other parents and children hung on its success or failure.

The Murphys had built their case around the lack of medical attention paid to their son and contra-indications after the first vaccination. After that injection, Daragh became feverish and his arm became swollen and stiff. His mother noticed that he used his arm less and less. When the time came for the second injection, the doctor asked no questions about how Daragh had reacted to the first injection—which she was supposed to do—and administered the second vaccination shot. That evening, Daragh's right arm became very stiff. He became feverish and emitted high-pitched screams. Two days later his eyes started rolling in his head. Daragh's parents brought him to a specialist who said the baby should not have the third whooping cough injection. But the damage had been done and he never recovered. Thereafter, he was physically retarded and his sight impaired.

The defence brought in a neurologist from Glasgow, John Stephenson, who examined Daragh and said that the boy had a brain defect from before birth. This doctor also said that there was no such thing as a contra-indication to the pertussis vaccine. The jury decided that the vaccination was not responsible for the child's disability. The Eastern Health Board did not press for costs against the parents of the boy. That failure, however, showed just how difficult it would be to win a case with so many experts with conflicting views. It was a major blow to the Association as it scared parents from trying to get justice in the courts for their damaged children.

At the same time there was a huge increase in cases of whooping cough. There were 668 cases in Ireland between July and November 1977, compared to 71 cases between the previous July and September. Then again, in the three years ending June 1977 there had been two deaths from whooping cough, compared to five deaths in the previous three years. As Dr Richard Halvorsen wrote in his book *The Truth about Vaccines*, the sudden fall-off in use of the pertussis vaccine after it had been in wide use for years created a test of its own to see how effective the vaccine really was:

In the 1970s, the immunisation rates in three similar countries, France, Britain and West Germany varied between 95 per cent and 10 per cent. However, the death rate from whooping cough remained the same in all three countries, suggesting the vaccine made no difference. Between 1981 and 1983, when no whooping cough vaccinations were given in Sweden, there were only three deaths, and two of these were in severely disabled children.

But scares and concerns abounded. Haughey made a statement saying some of the parents who had been afraid to get the whooping cough vaccine for their children had changed their minds. He said there was a new demand for a pertussis vaccine alone—for children who had already been vaccinated against tetanus and diphtheria—but that this did not exist. So the pressure was back on parents to get the three-in-one.

In April 1978, P.W. Flanagan of the Department of Health attended a special meeting of the Association at the Central Hotel. There, he explained the government's position and listened to the complaints and reservations of our members about the way the panel was being established. The word that came back was that Haughey didn't change his mind, and that he saw no point in meeting us again. The expert panel put advertisements in the papers inviting people to present their cases.

People were in dire circumstances, and the view that there was likely to be some form of compensation at the end of the tribunal meant that a lot of people brought the cases of their children to the expert panel. The loss of the Murphy court case left many parents feeling there was no hope in the courts and therefore no other choice but the panel for those who didn't want to battle on.

As happened in Ireland, the changed view of the whooping cough vaccine brought a public response in the UK. As opposed to Ireland, the British government took action. By early 1978, there was a huge increase in whooping cough in Great Britain and Northern Ireland. In the first six months of the year there were over 30,000 cases, including nine deaths. People had been frightened off the vaccine, and the government were desperate to win back the parents' confidence. By that time only three in ten babies in Britain were getting the pertussis vaccine. Labour's Jack Ashley, who had been supporting Rosemary Fox for years, said:

"The government has a particular responsibility to compensate children destroyed by vaccine because they are vaccinated primarily for the benefit of others who are too young to be vaccinated themselves. The main benefit is to the community at large, yet all the risk is to the individual."

In May, the British Health Secretary announced that an immediate £10,000 payment would be made to people who had suffered damage as a result of vaccination. This figure would be deducted from whatever compensation sum was eventually agreed in each case, but was an immediate gesture to help the people involved. The action was welcomed by most people.

In Ireland, meanwhile, I had written to Charlie Haughey again seeking a meeting about the expert panel. He wrote back saying he saw no point in a further meeting. I wrote back again, pointing out that he had sat with me when we faced Brendan Corish. After that meeting the Department of Health issued a statement saying:

The Tánaiste agreed to set up an expert medical group in agreement with the Association to assess each case where a claim for compensation may be made and a further discussion will be held when the studies are completed.

Haughey still didn't change his mind. In response to the Association's view that it must have a voice on the panel, P.W. Flanagan wrote to us saying:

To include on the group any doctor who had a commitment to one view or the other on the issue of vaccination damage would be to create a situation in which the group would become a forum for debate rather than become a scientific attempt to assess whether claims of damage could be attributed to vaccination.

So no voice from our side or else it would be a 'debate'. So what did they do? They appointed the Chief Medical Officer, Brendan O'Donnell—the man in charge of seeing that vaccinations were being carried out throughout the country—to the panel. Charlie had become the next politician to turn his back on us. Politicians in power are different animals from those trying to get power.

But I wasn't quitting. I was still fighting to have our case heard fairly. It seemed to me that politicians, like doctors, had only one wish: to make the problem go away. But I wasn't going to let that happen. I was going to fight them every step of the way to get justice for Alan.

Then absolutely everything came to a halt when my daughter Renee, 14 months old, was diagnosed with a brain tumour.

Chapter 4 ∾

| RENEE

Renee was a crying baby. There were times when she would be lying on the floor and she would be screaming. Kevin said she was spoiled and that I was over-attentive. He used to tell me to let her cry. He wouldn't want me to pick her up, and he said I was being over-fussy with her because of what had happened to Alan. He said that when she threw a tantrum and lay on the floor screaming, I would pick her up and start loving her and that only encouraged her to be bold. In truth, I didn't care if Renee was bold. I loved her so much I didn't care if I was spoiling her.

But after a while I felt there was something not right. When I'd call her, she would turn her head in an odd way. When I'd say this to Kevin, he would dismiss it.

"What do you mean she turns her head odd?" he'd say.

"It's as if she makes a conscious decision. Her whole body moves around. Call her." Kevin would call her and when he'd see the way she moved, he would still dismiss my worries. Everyone thought that, after what had happened to Alan, I couldn't trust that everything would be okay with my new baby.

I was going to doctors and all of them said I was worrying too much. I had reached the stage where I would never trust what one doctor told me, so I would always go to a different doctor because I was still worried about Renee. Eventually, one doctor suggested that I bring her to Crumlin Children's Hospital so that Dr Tempany could examine her. Tempany was one of the doctors looking after Alan.

When I went to him and told him my concerns, he said "Vera, will you please enjoy your child. You're paranoid. Everything is fine." I decided to take his word for it then, but a month later I went back to him and insisted he do tests. By then, Renee was starting to lose weight and she was losing her balance even when she was sitting. At first the doctor thought Renee had an ear infection. But he had an X-ray and a brain scan carried out on Renee to make sure there was no cause for concern. A few days later he called me and Kevin to come in and see him. I knew that was a bad sign and dreaded what he might say. Kevin and I went to the hospital and sat down with Tempany in his office. "It's not good news," he told us. "Renee has an inoperable brain tumour. It's cancerous."

My world fell apart at that moment. What was the worst thing that could happen? After Alan's brain damage, it was always heads that I worried about. And now here it was with my baby daughter—a cancerous tumour in her head. How could life be so cruel? I couldn't imagine a worse blow. The thought of what lay ahead was unbearable.

When we got home, I was in a shocking state. I went upstairs and fell into bed. The next day, Kevin told me a story that even in the depths of this situation I had to find funny. Kevin has never drunk alcohol, but after I went to bed he decided that for once in his life he would get drunk and knock himself into oblivion. He went into the living room with a bottle of whiskey. Because he had never taken alcohol, he figured that he might react very strongly and suddenly to it, but things were bad enough without his accidentally injuring himself if he fell over. So he set down cushions against dangerous corners like at the fireplace, and then sat himself down on cushions on the floor. He poured himself his first ever glass of whiskey and raised the glass to his mouth. When he smelt the whiskey it nearly turned his stomach, so he threw it down the sink and came to bed.

A surgeon agreed to operate on Renee. He warned us that he

believed the tumour was malignant and that the chances of a successful operation were low, but the choices were either to operate or to watch the tumour grow. The operation was carried out in the Richmond Hospital in Dublin on 12 September 1978. We brought Renee into the hospital the day before her operation. At that time the hospital had a lot of prefabricated buildings around it and Renee's ward was in one of those. I still have a picture of her in my mind. She was standing up at the back of the cot as I was leaving. I was going to the shop to get her lollipops and she was waving at me and she was laughing. It was the last time I saw her stand.

I remember sitting in a waiting room all the time Renee was going through the surgery. I wouldn't leave. I sat there thinking "She'll come through this. She'll come through this."

The surgeon met us after the operation and told us it had not been a success. I remember standing there with Kevin, and I was clutching something in my hand. I kept thinking, "I can't listen to any more of what you're saying." The surgeon told us that Renee would be paralysed on one side. I couldn't bear to hear any more. He said he had removed what he could of the tumour. He also reminded us that he had not expected success with the operation. When they operated on Renee, they found that the tumour was coiled into her brain stem.

I walked away. Kevin stayed and listened to the rest. As I found out many years later, Kevin was told that Renee did not have much longer to live. He didn't tell me at the time. He knew I would not have been able to handle it.

When Kevin came away from the surgeon's office, he went looking for me. He found me outside a doorway of the hospital, struggling with a man and woman who had pulled me away from what I had been doing. I had been standing there, slamming my head against a pebbledash stone wall. Blood was pouring down my face and I had broken my nose. I had lumps of grit in my face. They say I fractured my skull. All the skin was shredded on my forehead.

I was taken into casualty and they gave me an injection to calm me down. I remember them trying to pick the pieces of pebble and dirt out of my face as I lay there. I was feeling stinging pain, probably from the antiseptic they had put on me. But I had felt nothing when I was beating my head off the wall. My head was bandaged and I had two black eyes. When Kevin saw the state of me, he cried.

In that state, I went in to see Renee for the first time since her operation. All that kept going through my head was, this couldn't be true. This just couldn't be true. Her head was completely shaved. They had opened her head and a piece of her skull had been taken out. Because of the tumour she couldn't swallow and they had a device to take the fluid from her lungs. She was connected to drips.

Being numb was the only way I could react. I had no way of dealing with what was happening. I looked at her and all I could think was, why? Why is this happening?

I knew she was in pain. I knew the doctors were not sure if she would recover from the operation at all. In my mind, though, she was never going to die. I was going to get her fixed somehow or other. I would never leave her cot. I would sit at the side of the cot and hold her hand.

"If I leave her she'll die," I told everyone. "She can't die when I'm beside her." The nurses would come in and find me asleep, with my head resting on the cot. Kevin would try to convince me to go home, but I wouldn't. Sometimes they would carry me out in the middle of the night and Kevin would take me home. But I wouldn't be able to sleep then and I would go straight back to the hospital.

I saw everything they had to do to her. The worst thing was the suturing, where Renee would be choking and they had to drain her chest. Months went by with Renee lying there lifeless. She had hydrocephalus—fluid was building up on her brain and doctors had talked with Kevin about the possibility of another operation to deal with that. But it was decided not to put her through another operation.

Then, to our delight and to the surprise of the doctors, Renee started to rally around in December. She started to talk again. She was becoming alert. She couldn't use one side, but she would talk with me and she was completely aware of what had happened to her. She started to eat normal food.

After a while she was moved to Crumlin Hospital. One day there I saw Dr Tempany again and he admitted there was nothing more medicine could do for Renee.

"Medicine destroyed my son," I said, "and now you're telling me medicine can't save my daughter. The whole profession makes me sick to my stomach."

In February 1979 I contacted the neurologist John Wilson at the Ormond Street Hospital in London. He referred me to a surgeon who would see if there was a way of dealing with Renee's hydrocephalus. I flew to London with Renee, and this surgeon said he would operate on her and insert a shunt—a device that could drain the fluid from Renee's brain.

The operation was carried out and I stayed in London for a few weeks until Renee was well enough to travel. I was holding her in my arms on the aeroplane back to Dublin when I realised my hand was wet. Then I noticed that the bandaging around Renee's head was wet—the shunt had started to leak. A phone call was made from the plane to Dr Tempany in Dublin telling him the situation, and when we landed there was an ambulance waiting to speed Renee to Crumlin Hospital. She was rushed into the operating theatre and the shunt was removed.

A course of radiotherapy was begun at St Luke's Hospital to try and halt the growth of the tumour. This made Renee very sick and she was vomiting a lot. At the end of the course of radiotherapy, she was kept on steroids. Such was my little daughter's life.

Late that summer, Pope John Paul II made his visit to Ireland. Friends told me there would be an event where the Pope would be blessing sick children. A priest came to me, asking if I would bring Alan and Renee to be blessed by the Pope and that it would be televised. I said no and he asked why.

"I've pleaded with heaven," I said. "I've been in Lourdes. I've prayed and prayed. What's the Pope going to do? Bless two hopeless cases just to make good television?" But I did take Renee to the Phoenix Park when the Pope celebrated Mass there. I hadn't stopped pleading with God for her life: I just didn't want to be put on show for the country.

Renee was very intelligent. Sometimes she would say to me, "Mammy, stop crying."

"I'm not crying."

"I know you're crying. I can see you shaking."

I think of it as the worst nightmare anyone could have. I know I have blocked out a lot of it and I don't like writing about it. There were several times when she was at death's door, and I always believed I was the one who pulled her back because I would not let her go. I swore I would never let go of her. I believed that God would try to sneak her away from me if I wasn't there with her. It was then that I started pleading with God not to take her. When I look back now, I realise I had become deranged.

I was praying and praying for Renee. I wanted help from heaven to save my daughter. One person I latched on to was Father Charles, a very holy priest who was buried in Mount Argus church on the southside of Dublin. I was somehow convinced that Fr Charles was going to cure Renee. I would go to the church and into the right-hand side was his tomb. I would pray to him, and I would give him any money I had. Sometimes I walked out of the church with not even my bus fare home. I thought if I put a lot of money in, then he might listen. Sometimes I would leave myself without a penny for the next day, but it didn't matter—I was convinced he was going to cure Renee.

One day I saw a priest in the church and I told him my daughter was not going to live unless I could get a relic from Fr

Charles. The priest said he wasn't able to help, because Fr Charles had not been beatified. I said it didn't matter, and that I was convinced a relic would cure Renee.

The next day I went to the church. The priest had a piece of cloth from the habit of Fr Charles. He had opened up the tomb and cut out a piece for me. For all I know it was just any old piece of cloth and the priest had done this to try and put my mind at rest. In any event, I danced away and off to the Richmond Hospital. I was elated because I was absolutely certain Renee would be cured. I put the relic at the back of her cot and waited.

There was no miracle.

I then cursed Fr Charles from a height because he had let me down and I moved on to look for another saint. The next was St Theresa; after that Padre Pio. With each one it was the same: I would give them so many weeks to perform the miracle, but when the miracle didn't happen I would move on.

I used to walk from the Richmond Hospital to a church around the corner. Outside the church was a grotto with a statue of Our Lady. I would kneel at that grotto until I was in agony with pain in my knees. I would be thinking that if I said three rosaries she might hear me. And I would pray and pray, but nothing happened. I would speak out loud to the statues, begging for Renee's life.

I had one truly odd experience. Inside the same church was a statue of the saint known as the Little Flower. I prayed to her and I said, 'You were only young when you died, and I know you were really here on Earth. So let me peep into heaven. If I know there's really a heaven, then I might be able to give Renee up. But I have to know there's a heaven for her.'

When I was back in Renee's room after that, there was a knock at the door. A woman was there—a woman I had never met before—and she had a little casket with a yellow rose in it.

"I have to bless your child with this," she said.

"Where did you get it?" I asked.

"A holy nun died, and as I was standing at the coffin, a thought came to my head that I should bring this to you. The nun and I had talked about you and your child, and the thought came to my head to bring this flower to your child and bless her."

This was minutes after my walking back from the church where I had talked to the Little Flower statue.

"I don't want to touch that flower," I said. "You bless her with it."

The woman blessed Renee with the flower and placed it by her cot. I went home and told Kevin what had happened. "Do you think the Little Flower heard me?" I asked him. "Was that a sign?" When I mentioned what had happened to some friends, they passed the word on to the local parish priest. He called to me and said he was arranging a special Mass for the Little Flower and Renee.

"Coincidences like that don't happen, Vera," he told me. If there was any chance of help from above, he wanted to protect and support it. My friends and neighbours came to the Mass. Candles were lit around the feet of a statue of the Little Flower. I let myself hope that this time something might happen. But there was no change in Renee and no glimpse into heaven.

———

Life for other people was going along with blessed normality, and sometimes I found that hard. My brother Finbarr's wife gave birth to a baby boy at the Rotunda Hospital and I went up to visit her and congratulate them. They were, of course, delighted with their new baby and were talking about what name they would choose. I wished them well. As I was walking out of the hospital, I stopped at the top of the stone stairway exit and all I could think was, how can all this be happening to me? This is so unfair. I then threw myself down the stairs. When I got up I was just bruised and hurt though I wanted to be dead. I left the hospital and walked down the middle of O'Connell Street with traffic going past me. I thought, I'll fall under the next bus. But that one would pass. I didn't have the courage. In the end I couldn't do it. I wanted to die, but Renee needed me.

As the end of 1979 approached, Renee had spent over a year of her little life in hospital. On Christmas Day 1979, Kevin and I went in to Crumlin Hospital and brought Renee home. She was as well as the doctors could make her, and we wanted to have our time with her.

We had our fun times together as a family, Kevin and I trying always not to think about what lay ahead. Despite all that was happening to Renee, she was a happy child. I remember one time I had settled her in bed and I was downstairs with Kevin and I heard her. She was playing with a rattle toy strung across the top of her cot and she was singing. I listened to her and I said to Kevin, "Isn't that magical?"

I couldn't bear to see Alan and Renee together. I had to have them in separate rooms. If I was finished doing something with one and had to tend to the other, I would have someone take one child to the living room before I brought the other child into the kitchen.

Because Renee was paralysed on one side, there was a special buggy wheelchair made for her with a support that kept her head upright. Sometimes on Sunday afternoons Kevin and I would go for a stroll along the Clontarf promenade, each of us pushing a wheelchair. I would wheel Alan and Kevin would wheel Renee because her buggy was heavier. They both loved ice cream—Alan enjoyed it, and it was something that Renee could swallow easily. One Sunday afternoon we went into Cafolla's Café on O'Connell Street to give them a treat. We were stopped by the manager of the café as we entered. He told us we couldn't be allowed in because we would be blocking the aisles for other customers. Kevin and I almost cried—that someone could take such an attitude. "You can take a tub and feed them outside if you like," the manager said, "but you can't bring them in."

Kevin went to the newspapers about it, and the story was on the front pages. The manager apologised. But we had felt so humiliated that we rarely tried bringing our children into places like that afterwards. Fortunately for people today, things are a little better.

———

I had gone to Lourdes with Alan twice. When Renee became sick I decided I would go with her once. She was starting to get stronger, and the doctors agreed that she could manage the journey. Kevin and I travelled again to that sad place to join all the people begging for a miracle.

When it was my turn to walk with Renee into the baths, I'll always remember the look on Kevin's face. I looked up at him and he had a look of absolute desperation. What struck me was that I knew the desperation was for me rather than for her. A terribly sad thing happened. There were women in the baths who recognised me from my trips with Alan. They saw me there with another hopeless case, and word went out. An announcement called for everyone in the basilica to pray while Renee was dipped in the water. I could hear this outpouring of prayer for her. I don't know how I managed to stand there in the baths and then walk to the statue and kiss its feet and walk away from there with my child in my arms. I remember thinking, if ever there's going to be a miracle, it's going to happen now.

There was no miracle.

I kept asking why. What had Kevin or I done that there was to be no miracle for us? I walked to Kevin and he put his arms around me.

"Come on, it's okay," he said. We walked away together with the people watching us.

"Get me out of here," I said. When I got away from there I cried and cried until I couldn't cry any more.

There were other events in Lourdes, and even though my heart was broken I was still thinking, maybe if I go in a procession there will be a miracle or maybe if I go to the blessings of the sick. So I attended all the events. I walked in the processions and I sang the hymns and I pleaded with God and his mother.

One day it was very hot and there were thousands gathered: loads of people in wheelchairs and on stretchers. A steward noticed me with Renee and ushered me down beside the grotto. Kevin stood back. He wanted to make room for other sick people. I stood at the foot of the statue in the grotto and looked up. I felt that if I started to cry I would never stop. A hand reached out to me. It was a very old woman. She just held my hand and smiled. Somehow she gave me the strength not to fall asunder, but I remember looking at her and thinking, why are you here? My child is 2 years old and you are nearly 80. Is that fair? And yet somehow I know that woman gave me some kind of strength that kept me together.

I didn't know what to say to God. I thought that if he wanted Renee to be better then she would be better, so if I was asking him then I was just annoying him. But then I thought that if I didn't ask enough then he would think I didn't care and he would take her. My head was in constant turmoil with all these thoughts. Was it selfish of me to want Renee better? God knows everything, so if he wanted her then he wanted her for a reason.

One day, at one of the gatherings, a woman standing close to me started screaming. She was blind and she cried out that she could see. I immediately thought, if that's true then Our Lady was standing right there, so why didn't she put her hand on a child instead of an adult? I visited the place where they display photographs and proof of miracles. Miracles do happen there, but I could never understand why I never got help from heaven for Renee. We left Lourdes, Renee not granted a miracle, and again I swore I would never return. Again, I was wrong.

Something happened that ended my pleading with God. Once, when Renee was in Crumlin Hospital, I was wheeling her around the corridors. She said, "Stop at the man."

"What man?" I asked.

"The man that I do see," she said.

What I discovered was that she wanted me to bring her to a statue of the Sacred Heart at the end of the corridor.

"Is that the man?" I asked her.

"Yes. I want to say hello to him. He says hello to me." I stood with my daughter in her wheelchair at the statue of the Sacred Heart. What was happening? Why did God want my child?

Sometime later I was with Renee at home. I was looking at her, with her head slumped down, and I got on my knees and I pleaded to God.

"Please don't take this child," I prayed. "There are children dying and unwanted and abused all over the world. I adore this child. Don't take her."

Renee suddenly lifted her head perfectly upright and turned around.

"Hello, man," she said.

Goose pimples stood out all over my skin and I froze.

"I'm really good today, man," she said. I was afraid to move. My whole body shook. It only lasted for a few seconds.

"Bye, man," Renee said. And her head slumped back down to the way it usually was.

From that moment on I felt it was out of my hands. Whatever Renee was born for, or whatever the reasons for her illness, I could never know. What was happening was beyond my powers. If God was there but wasn't fixing her, then he was letting her die. And if he was letting her die, then I was going to become someone who would hate him like he could never imagine.

Kevin and I made the best of our time with Renee. I had become really exhausted, though, and Kevin convinced me to join him on a short trip he was making to the US on business. I agreed, and arrangements were made to take care of Renee and Alan. Through a social worker, a place was arranged for Alan in a home called St Anthony's.

And what happened? The 'caring' medical profession showed its true colours yet again. Even though my thoughts were far away from the whole vaccination debate, I was still being hounded for lifting that lid. Dr Neil O'Doherty was the paediatrician at the home and he refused to have Alan in his care. O'Doherty had never forgiven us for challenging his diagnosis of Alan. That grudge was more important to him than the welfare of a child or helping parents with two incurable children. He wrote, on 13 May 1980, a letter to the secretary of the Children's Hospital on its headed paper stating: 'This is to confirm my conversation of today to the effect that I will not have this boy either as my in-patient or out-patient in this Hospital or at St Anthony's Hospital, ever. The slight confusion that arose the other day when I was telephoned at St Michael's House is due to the fact that although I recognised the name right away, for the moment the previous overtones of this case escaped me.' This was the behaviour of a man who had supposedly dedicated his professional life to the welfare of children. An alternative arrangement was made by the social worker and I made the trip with Kevin.

———

The most serious crisis of all then came. Alan got mumps and before we realised what he had, Renee caught them too. It made her sicker than she had ever been and she was taken back into hospital. The mumps could kill her because she would not be able to swallow. Since the time she was diagnosed there had been crises and black times, but this looked like the end for Renee.

By that stage I would take anything the doctors gave me. Give me sleeping tablets. I'll take them. Give me anti-depressants. I'll take them. I would take anything that would keep me going for Renee. I rarely drink anything stronger than a glass of wine, but I remember deciding one day that I'd have a brandy. I drank the brandy to wash down whichever pill I was due to take at that time of the day. I had another brandy after that, and another pill. It helped me feel better. Then off I went to see Renee.

I floated along the corridor of Crumlin Hospital not realising that, between the alcohol and the medication, I had overdosed. I reached Renee's room, saw her in her cot, and then slumped to the ground. I was told later that when a nurse opened my eyes and saw my pupils so dilated, they believed I was dying. I was put on a trolley and sped down the corridors, bashing the doors open, to get me to the emergency ward. They needed to pump my stomach, but this being a children's hospital, the tubes were not long enough. I was rushed by ambulance to St Vincent's Hospital.

At that hospital I was described as an 'attempted suicide'. A man came to my room—a counsellor. He was there to start giving me psychotherapy and find out why I had tried to take my life. When I explained what had happened, he said that no one could take that kind of beating without help. He said I needed to stay at the hospital for a few days. "If you were my daughter," he said, "I wouldn't let you out of here."

They moved me to the psychiatric ward. I was back in mental care again. On one side was a woman who had cut her wrists, and on the other side a woman with all kinds of problems. I was there purely brokenhearted and smashed to bits.

The next morning I was brought in to occupational therapy. I asked what this was for.

"You need to keep yourself occupied," they explained.

"Doing what?" I asked.

I agreed to go along with whatever they thought would be good for me. I was brought into a room where all the patients were sitting around in a circle. They started talking to each other about their problems, but from my point of view at that time what they talked about was ridiculous. One woman talked about not being understood by her father; another talked about her marriage having broken up. I didn't know what I was doing there. I was surrounded by psychiatric cases and couldn't understand what their problems were. I was there because I was losing a second child.

"I don't want to participate in this," I told a nurse. "I don't want to discuss my life. Is there anything else I can do?" But I had to stay in this group.

They later changed over to playing a word/picture game. I was asked to keep the score. They would, for instance, put up a picture of an actor and the people in the group would be asked if they could remember the actor's name or what films the actor had been in. That was my morning of occupational therapy.

We had lunch after that, and in the afternoon there was another session of group therapy. At this stage I was just feeling amused and distracted listening to these stories. But after that session, I was asked to join the group who were making baskets.

"It's easy to do and very therapeutic," I was told.

"If I want a fucking basket, I'll buy a fucking basket," was my response.

"But you can't just sit there and do nothing," they said.

"Of course I can. Give me a good book and I'll have a read."

"You need to be working with your hands."

"I am not weaving baskets. I'm going back to my room."

I went back to my room. At that stage I had been there one night, and had already decided I was getting out of there. I knew that whatever chance I had of surviving the grief, I stood no chance of doing so in that place. I phoned Kevin and found out that he had been talking with family and friends and he had decided that I had to leave the hospital.

"Get me out of here quick," I told him.

"I was already on my way," he said. "You don't need to be there and I'm getting you out."

We sat in an office with the doctors in charge of the ward. They told Kevin he was making a terrible mistake because they believed I needed care.

"She cannot cope with what's happened to her out there," they said.

"There's 24 hours in a day," Kevin said, "And out of that 24 hours you might be able to help Vera for half an hour, but the rest of the time here will destroy her."

I came home with Kevin and a load of different pills the hospital had given me. Kevin and I knelt down and said the 'Our Father' together. Then we flushed all the pills down the toilet. I took no more pills while Renee was alive.

———

Renee's condition became worse and she was taken back into Crumlin Hospital a few days after her 3rd birthday. The fluid was building up more and more on her brain and she was having difficulty swallowing and breathing. After a few weeks the doctors said they needed to operate. They also warned that this time there was a lot of risk, but it was the only hope, and we agreed.

At first it seemed like the operation had been a success. Then Renee started taking fits and was in ever more distress because she couldn't breathe. They had an oxygen tent over her head. I got my hand under the tent and I held her hand. The nurses were coming in, and I knew by the looks they were giving Kevin that they knew she was dying. I was still determined that Renee would not die. I sat in that chair holding her hand and keeping her alive.

Then—I swear this is true—I felt someone take my hand and just lead me out of the room. Kevin and my sister Anna watched me and couldn't understand what was going on. I was led to a room beside where Renee lay dying, and I was sat down. I felt this hand cover my eyes, and I was instantly asleep.

Kevin woke me. I have no idea how long I slept. "Vera, she's going."

I went back into Renee's room and I put my hand on Renee's chest.

"She's gone," a nurse said.

"While I was out of the room?"

"She couldn't go while you were there."

Renee died at 5.25 in the morning on 20 July 1980, six weeks after her 3rd birthday.

I heard them talking about taking her to a mortuary, and I was telling them to bring that teddy bear and that doll because she liked them. Kevin led me away. I was walking down the hospital corridor and I saw a statue of Our Lady. I spat at it. I swore I would never pray again and that I would never go into a church again.

When we got home, I remember hearing Kevin in another room, breaking his heart crying. I went in to him.

"It's okay," I said. "I'll help you. Don't fall to pieces. I'll help you."

He stopped crying. But how could I help him?

———

The funeral was terrible and I don't even want to try to remember it. In fact, that time is a complete blank for me. I remember every detail up to the time I saw Renee in the coffin. Everything after that is gone from my mind. It's strange. I don't remember standing at Renee's graveside. The only connected memory I have is that, a couple of days after the funeral I found myself in a different graveyard—a small one in Clontarf not far from where we live—kneeling at a small unmarked grave. A man came along and asked me if I was all right. Somehow I was convinced that Renee was buried there. I don't know what kind of state I was in, but the man offered to take me home and I said I wouldn't leave my daughter's grave. He must have got Kevin's phone number from me, because eventually Kevin came to me at this graveside.

"Isn't Renee in here?" I said to him. He took me in his arms and brought me home.

When Renee died I really did have a breakdown. I used to roll up in a ball in the foetal position, and I had no will to live. I wanted to die. I couldn't live without Renee. I felt I had to follow her. I had a cardigan of Renee's that she had puked on. I had hidden this, and I would take it out from time to time so I could smell it. I had snips of her hair hidden also and would take these out. I would lie in the bed smelling the cardigan. By then I think Kevin was terrified that if I was taken back into a psychiatric institution I would never come out.

At that time, I would lie in bed and think there were insects crawling over my skin. I thought someone was pulling my eyes into the back of my head with strings. I thought my teeth were falling out. "You're having a nervous breakdown," I remember the doctor shouting at me as I was lying in bed. I thought to myself that I had sworn never to have a breakdown, and I was sure I was feeling all this because the drugs I had been given were poisoning me. The doctor told Kevin that I needed to be shifted to hospital, but Kevin refused. The doctor said he was giving me an injection that would knock an elephant out for 48 hours. I remained awake.

Kevin realised I was in a terrible state and he phoned my aunt, Vera Lynch. She came straight away. She was the person who pulled me through. I was in bed and told Vera that I wanted to get downstairs. I wanted Kevin to see that I could get out of the bed. Vera helped me, but I had to go down the stairs on my bum because I felt I had no legs. We sat up all night talking—Vera, her husband, Kevin and me. The injection never put me to sleep. When the doctor came to see me the next day, I told him I still had not slept. I also told him that if he thought I was having a nervous breakdown he was wrong.

"You can go away and don't come back. I'll postpone the breakdown for another while," I said.

I wasn't always able to take care of Alan in the months after Renee's death, and sometimes he had to stay for a while in care. I went up to see him one day and recognised the buggy wheelchair that had been built for Renee. I walked towards it as a nurse turned the buggy around. Alan was sitting in the buggy. It turned out that Kevin had given the buggy to the home and someone—not knowing the direct connection—had put Alan in it. I told them to take Alan out of the buggy and to never let me see it again. I really wanted to take a hatchet to the thing.

Up to the time Renee died I was having black-outs. I was told later that this was a kind of safety valve. I was walking between sanity and insanity and just couldn't be pushed any further. After her death, I was living by what I had sworn to God—that I would hate him and be his worst enemy. I used to dream of talking with the Devil, and I used to say to God in my mind, 'That shook you. Now I'm the Devil's friend.' I told God I would be evil and that he would be sorry he took Renee. I was like a crazy woman. I was at war with God. I burned or threw out every religious ornament, relic or picture in our home and I emptied holy water down the toilet. I may well have thrown out some rare relics sent to me by people around the country who knew what had happened with Renee and were trying to help.

I had a cross that a holy man had given me long before, and one day I picked it up and it flew across the room.

"Did you see that?" I said to Kevin. "The cross flew away from me because God knows I'm talking with the Devil."

"Vera, you threw the cross yourself," he said.

Kevin asked a priest to come to the house and talk with me. The priest came and blessed me. I told him that I wanted to be friends with the Devil. "I'm giving him my soul, too," I said.

This was going on for months. I was losing weight and I was on heavy medication. I was willing myself to die. Towards the end of the year, my sister Nuala was home from London and I told her I was dying.

"I haven't had a period for months," I said. "It's because I'm willing myself to die. Renee wants me to be with her."

"Could you be pregnant?" Nuala asked me, and I started laughing.

"Not unless it's the Immaculate Conception," I said.

Nuala insisted that I get a pregnancy test. It was positive. I went to see Dr Tempany and told him about my situation. He held me by the shoulders and looked me in the eyes.

"In all my years as a doctor," he said, "I've never come across anything so extraordinary. Your physical and mental condition should stop your becoming pregnant. The medication you're on stops ovulation. If you're pregnant, it's the hand of God. There's no medical explanation."

"If I'm pregnant," I said, "I'm going to abort this child as my revenge on God. I'm going to kill this child because he took Renee."

I went for a scan. The doctor told me that the due date for the baby was 20 July—the day Renee died. I didn't know what to do. I could never have imagined I was pregnant. I had been popping pills and had been in a terrible condition. How could I know if this child would be all right?

A counsellor came out to the house to talk to me. I was full of anger with God and I didn't want to have the child God was giving me—I wanted the child he had taken away from me. I know Kevin would have stopped me from having an abortion, but I had so much hate then that if I had found a way of doing it, I would have had one. I went on with the pregnancy, but I didn't welcome it. It was months before I came to accept that I was going to have another child. People were trying to change my attitude, saying "God is giving you back this new life", and I would just curse him. I was deranged with anger.

I wouldn't go into Mount Carmel Hospital for the delivery,

because that was where Renee was born. It was suggested that I go to Holles Street for the birth and I went to see what it was like. I walked around and then said, "I'd never come in here. It's full of holy pictures." I went instead to the Coombe Hospital simply because I didn't see holy pictures around.

When I arrived at the hospital for the delivery, there were painters working on the corridor. As I passed them I had a massive contraction and the nurse who was walking with me put her hand on my stomach. I hit her. That's the frame of mind I was in.

At that time fathers were not allowed to be present at births. Kevin had told the nurses that he would be present at the birth and they had told him it wasn't possible. Kevin knew I didn't want to go through the birth without him. So when the matron refused to let Kevin into the theatre, he said, "I either go through you or you get out of my way." Kevin doesn't often get aggressive with people, but he would do anything for me. The matron knew he meant what he said. Kevin attended the birth.

I gave birth to a baby girl on 27 July 1981, a week after the first anniversary of Renee's death. When the baby was born, I wouldn't look at her. They asked if I wanted to hold her and I refused.

"I tell you what I'll do," I said. "When you check out—whether it takes a week or a day—that she's healthy and she's well and there's nothing wrong with her, then I might hold her. But now I don't even want to see her."

So they took the baby away and I was wheeled back to a ward full of women with their newborn babies. Hours later a doctor came to me.

"Mrs Duffy," he said, "you've had a wonderful baby girl and we're wondering if this child is to go up for adoption."

"What do you mean, adoption?"

"Well, I believe you don't want to hold her and you haven't even seen her." He sat down beside me. "I know your history, Vera. But we've done all the tests and you've a beautiful healthy little girl." Then he said, joking of course, "So does this child go up for adoption or does this child have a mother?"

"Bring her in," I said. A nurse carried her in. I took the baby in my arms. The nurse and doctor both cried. Needless to say, once I saw her and held her, I loved her completely. So began the life of my daughter Olga, who is a fine, healthy and gifted young woman.

———

Many years later there was a new huge medical scandal. It was revealed that, around the time of Renee's death and without the knowledge of parents, internal organs were being removed from deceased children in Our Lady's Hospital for Sick Children in Crumlin. I phoned up the hospital and ended up—by great coincidence—speaking with a woman I had known years before.

"If they had done it," she assured me, "they'd be telling you now."

"You really don't expect me to believe that," was my reply.

In the end, I received a letter from the hospital assuring me that they had not touched Renee. But over the years I have seen little proof that the medical profession can be believed, so I took no great comfort from their reassurance.

| THE TRUTH

The battle for justice for vaccine-damaged children had carried on without me. Throughout Renee's illness and death, I had no thought or energy for anything but my own family. When Olga was born, I decided it was time for me to get my own life together and concentrate on my family. It was up to others to keep on banging against the brick wall.

In 1982, after four years, there was still no announcement made about the findings of the panel of experts. Fifty-four cases had been brought to the panel. *Irish Independent* journalist Brian McDonald has since uncovered research showing that, around the time of the establishing of the expert panel to consider pertussis vaccine brain-damage cases, senior Department of Health officials had said it would be 'inconsistent and inconclusive' not to concede proper compensation. These officials recommended in a written memo that a board of assessors be set up to decide on the issue of compensation. So they knew the truth. But were they going to act on it?

In May 1982 a group of parents went to see Dr Michael D. Woods, the Minister for Health. He promised that the findings would be published, a statement made and that he would contact parents individually. By that time only about 40 per cent of babies in Ireland were being vaccinated against whooping cough. Parents now had to sign consent forms before their babies were vaccinated, and doctors had to report any reactions to their supervising medical officers—two changes that were made as a

Alan loving all the attention, taking a good look at the photographer.

Both Tracey and Alan are fed up with this picture business! Tracey has a forced smile; Alan loves his soother.

Tracey and Alan again. Alan, staring at the camera, is very curious as to what is going on.

Alan on my lap; Tracey on Kevin's lap. I am telling the children to clap hands. Tracey obliges while Alan just looks on.

Alan loved his bouncing chair. He is wearing a brown and yellow knitted suit. I knitted all his clothes and booties.

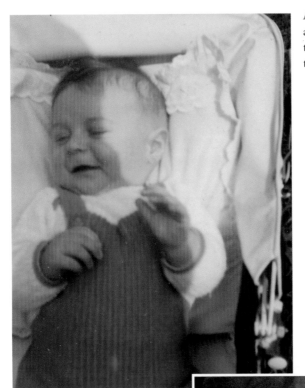

Alan in his pram, aged approximately two months, trying to shield his eyes from the sun.

Alan at the beach. But there was no enjoyment that day: this is Alan in a convulsion.

The picture tells it all: Alan has no idea what is happening. I hate this photo.

A day in the garden. Renee on the left, Alan centre and Tracey on the right. Renee died 11 months after this picture was taken.

Our Lady's Hospital for Sick Children, Crumlin, Dublin, where Alan was treated. (© *Collins Agency*)

Alan has now left my care. This photo was taken in St Michael's House, Ballymun.

Alan on his bed in St Michael's House, at about 17 years old here. I brought in a professional photographer (Tom Lawlor) to take these photographs. Alan would waste away for another five years until he died at the age of 22. It was too shocking to photograph his body then. I would never want to see it again.

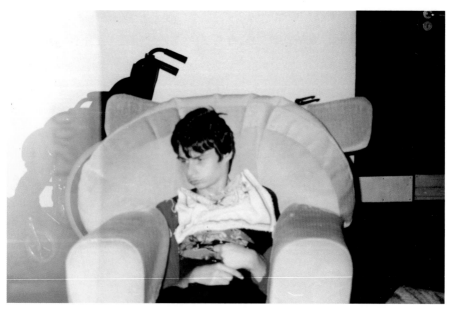

Alan pictured in St Michael's House. The brain damage was so bad that he never knew where he was.

December 1999: Another terrible disappointment. Why can't these judges see and understand what has been done to us? (© *Courtpix*)

My trip to Washington D.C. in 2000. I certainly got a huge eye-opener on that trip. Here I am with some of the lovely members of the National Vaccine Information Center.

The founders of the NVIC: Kathi Williams on the left, with Barbara Loe Fisher, centre. I am on the right. These two wonderful people opened my mind and taught me a great deal. I hated having to return to Ireland.

Arriving at the Supreme Court in 2001. Kevin made me smile, saying, "We will get there eventually." My daughter Olga takes my 'bad' side to help. We certainly walked in there with loads of hope—but it was not to be. (© *Collins Agency*)

April 2006: In hospital for more steroids to help my multiple sclerosis. (© *Irish Times*)

September 2008: Decision day at the Coroner's Court. My two wonderful daughters, Tracey and Olga, and two sons, Kevin Junior and Karl. Other members of my family, including Martin Duffy who had flown in from Berlin, came to support me that day. We had just finished a long meeting with our senior counsel. Kevin and I felt that Dr Brian Farrell, the city coroner, would do the right thing. (© *Collins Agency*)

Gerard Hogan, Senior Counsel. (© *Courtpix*)

Dublin City Coroner Dr Brian Farrell. (© *Courtpix*)

The coroner's hands were tied; I was totally devastated. The inquest opened on 4 December 1997 and concluded on 22 September 2008. But after almost 12 years, the truth still cannot be written on Alan's death certificate. He died of 'aspirational pneumonia'. It was strange that it all finished on the 22nd: Alan had died at the age of 22. (© *Collins Agency*)

result of the outcry caused by our Association, and changes that would have saved Alan's life if they had been in place when I brought him to be vaccinated. On the other hand, there had been a steep rise in the incidence of whooping cough in 1981. The problem was that now, instead of sacrificial lambs like Alan as a hidden cost of mass vaccination, people had become frightened by all the uncertainty, and the disease had the chance to spread.

In July, a statement was issued by the government and 54 letters were sent out. The only difference with each letter was the name it was addressed to and a sentence stating either that the vaccine had not caused the damage, or that there was a 'reasonable probability' that it had. The letter mentioned some of the symptoms reported and said 'as these are not uncommon occurrences also in infants who have never been vaccinated the Group recognised that it would be impossible to prove absolutely a cause-and-effect relationship in any case and could therefore only base its findings on the balance of probability'.

Fourteen cases were told they could receive £10,000 but could not—unlike the parents in the UK who had been given this sum years before—seek further compensation. The Irish government was going to pay out 'shut up' money to the parents of these victims. After seven years of campaigning, these parents got that letter and a brick wall. There was no means of appeal, and parents were not allowed access to the medical files from the expert panel. The panel members were: Dr Brendan O'Donnell, the Dublin Chief Medical Officer; Dr Edward Tempany (the paediatrician in Our Lady's Children's Hospital who had treated Alan and Renee); and Dr S.F. Murphy, a neurologist at Jervis Street and St Vincent's Hospital in Dublin.

To add further insult, Woods emphasised in his statement that 'there is no conclusive evidence that the vaccination caused the disability in any of the persons'. He said that research had shown a possible risk to one in 310,000 vaccines, a figure dismissed by Prof. Gordon Stewart, who said the risk was much higher. The

Minister's statement ended by advising all parents to have their children vaccinated against whooping cough because the benefits outweighed the risks. After all those years of campaigning, this was the government's response. They stonewalled us, and then they broke the will of people struggling to care for their brain-damaged children. Even with the 14 cases being offered money, the truth was being dodged with the 'reasonable probability' line—as if the government was giving these parents a hand-out.

So what had happened to the babies vaccinated in these cases? Always the basic pattern was the same: perfectly healthy babies suffering fits and convulsions after the injections. Often the parents were expressing their concerns and the doctors went on jabbing their needles regardless. Take the case of Noel Thornton. Noel was a perfectly healthy child of a year and ten months—talking and playing football—when he was given his first vaccination. That night he was having screaming fits. The doctor gave him the following two vaccinations despite the protests of his father, and Noel ended up dumb, near blind and paralysed. At first the diagnosis was polio, but this was later changed to encephalitis—brain damage. The experts could still say that Noel Thornton was not damaged by the vaccine.

Case after case was the same—the convulsions, the high-pitched scream, the withdrawal—but even that pattern was ignored.

Another case was that of Patrick O'Halloran. The hospital where he was born attested to the fact that he was perfectly healthy until he had the vaccine, and the doctor who administered the vaccine wrote a letter saying she believed the vaccine was the cause of his brain damage. The panel said they saw no evidence of vaccine damage.

Raymond Cousins experienced the same pattern of damage as Alan. There was also a history of asthma in his family, and an aunt of his had died of convulsions. He should not, in other words, have ever been given the vaccine, even by the manufacturer's own guidelines. After the damage to him became evident, his doctor later decided not to give the whooping cough vaccine to the mother's two subsequent children. The expert panel said there was no evidence of vaccine damage.

It all proved that I was right to have nothing to do with the 'expert panel' and that I was right not to have Alan examined by them. Patrick O'Halloran's mother, by the way, reported that the examination of her son took about ten minutes. "They asked me a couple of questions and tested Patrick's reflexes," she said.

The government just wanted the problem to go away. They wanted the mothers back queuing with their babies. They wanted people like us to be dismissed as foolish or as hard cases who could be given a hand-out but were not to be taken seriously. One family were going to take a court case against the Department of Health and went to a solicitor. When the solicitor started making enquiries, he was informed by the Department that if the family lost, the Department would press for legal costs estimated at about £50,000. The family decided not to proceed with the case. The shadow of the failed Daragh Murphy case in 1977 still hung over parents.

At that time I was still too low to be of help. People would call me for advice, but I had no energy left to join the fight. I was just trying to get my own life together again. Around the time of Renee's illness, Kevin and I had been trying to put a case together with a company of solicitors, but the papers just sat there gathering dust.

Fortunately, there was one mother whose case was accepted by the panel but who was not going to be shaken off so easily. After the Association for Vaccine-Damaged Children had been set up, a woman from Cork named Margaret Best came to me. Her son Kenneth had suffered in almost exactly the same way that my son Alan had. Kenneth was born in 1969 a perfectly healthy boy. He had some trouble with eczema, and the local doctor, Dr O'Keeffe, had prescribed an ointment. When Kenneth was five months old, and even though he was still being treated for his eczema, he was given his first dose of DPT vaccine. Within hours he suffered his first fit. Margaret Best, just like me, accepted the guidance of the medical professionals. "When I expressed concerns, I was told I was a fussy mother," she said. The two further vaccinations were given. By then Kenneth was massively damaged. That was the start of Margaret's battle for justice.

Margaret refused to accept the £10,000 offered to her. She told the *Evening Herald*'s Helen Rogers: "This letter from the Department about the findings of the expert panel is small consolation to me. Is this all I have been waiting for for over four years? I contacted the Minister's private secretary and he told me there was no question of compensation." She decided that she would bring the case to court. The cause of proving the dangers of the vaccination programme had found a great champion.

The Wellcome Foundation made the mistake of underestimating Margaret's intelligence. Margaret had a court order for discovery in preparing her case, and went into Wellcome with a woman friend. The two were ordinary country women and Wellcome didn't think twice about letting them look through files. Margaret and her friend spent hours photocopying files. Her most significant find was that the batch her son had been given had passed three standard tests but had been shown through a fourth test to be highly toxic. Yet Wellcome had released it on the market anyway. This was Margaret's crucial piece of rock solid evidence. In other cases—like Alan's—there wasn't the concrete information from files or other indisputable evidence that could be presented in court. It wasn't enough to believe in a cause and effect between the vaccine and the brain damage. Being able to prove that the batch was toxic was a way whereby this one incident, and not the vaccination programme as a whole, could be considered.

I was in constant contact with Margaret, and I gave her any help or advice I could. One time when we met in Cork, she pointed out two men who she said had been following her. She said they were from the Department of Health.

"They know who you are and they're watching to see that I don't hand you stuff," she said. "They'd do anything to stop me from bringing the case to court and they know you and what you have."

I walked over to them and asked them if they were lost. "No, we're not," they said and walked away. I went back to Margaret, who was laughing. Margaret had to put up with all kinds of stuff as she pursued her case, but she was a smart woman and would not be intimidated.

Eventually the case went to the High Court. The trial lasted 35 days. Margaret Best was bringing an action against the State, the Southern Health Board, Dr O'Keeffe and the Wellcome Foundation. When Niall O'Donohoe gave evidence, he stated that there could be no possible link between the vaccination and brain damage. The counsel quoted from a medical treatise that said the link was possible. O'Donohoe was asked if the words were familiar and he admitted they were. He had written them himself. "So how often do you change your opinion?" he was asked.

Margaret Best had a huge body of evidence, but her strongest piece of evidence was the discovery that the batch used on her son—batch 3741—was known by the manufacturer to be eight times more toxic than normal. Despite this evidence, the High Court judge ruled in January 1991 that a link between Kenneth's condition and the vaccine was not clearly established. In particular there was a conflict between the evidence of Kenneth's parents, who said he had his first fit within hours of the first vaccination in September 1969, and their doctor, whose notes when referring the case to a hospital in January 1970, said the parents had told him the fits had just recently begun.

It was devastating for Margaret. After years of gathering evidence, and with enormous legal costs, her case had been rejected. She and her legal team took the brave step of appealing to the Supreme Court. There, in June 1992, Chief Justice Finlay reviewed the case. He decided there was no case against the Health Board and the doctor, who had acted in good faith not knowing the vaccine was toxic, and he dismissed the case against the State. His key decision was that he allowed the evidence of the Best parents to have precedence over the note written by their doctor in January 1970. The Chief Justice accepted that Kenneth's fits had started within hours of his first injection, and said this was caused by the toxic batch. He ordered the case back to the High Court to establish a compensation figure. The following year, the High Court granted £2.75 million in damages.

I was delighted the day the Best case won. I felt that I had won. I danced up the Quays away from the courts. It proved that I had been right all along. But I hadn't won. The price of Margaret Best's victory was that she was sworn to silence on the information she had discovered in the Wellcome files. She had won because she had found reference to a particular toxic batch used on her son. This didn't open the door for other cases such as mine. If anything, it slammed the door shut because thereafter Wellcome knew their weak spot and the battle would have to be fought all over again.

When I contacted the solicitors who had won the Best case with regard to their taking on Alan's case, their response was, we're not facing that mountain again. In the following years I found the same thing over and over again: solicitors either didn't know how to take on such a case, or they could see no way of winning. In a sense, we were caught between two precedents: the Daragh Murphy case, where the case could be lost if the court believed there was any doubt about the direct and sole link between the vaccine and the damage, and the Best case, where only solid proof of a toxic batch had brought a positive verdict. Court cases in the UK had created a similar situation.

Kevin and I had a bag shop in Cork and I went down there most weekends. I often met Margaret on those trips as she was preparing her case. After she had won, I was staying at my usual hotel and the woman at the reception there told me that a BBC crew was staying there and had come to interview Margaret. Margaret hadn't mentioned it to me, and I felt that after she won her own case she stopped thinking about the battle that was still going on for others trying to prove the damage being caused by vaccines.

If I had been in her position and seen those documents, I would have released them to the press and the public, even if it meant that I would go to prison. I have never tried to get financial compensation for Alan. All I've ever wanted is the truth. I wish I knew what Margaret Best knows about the Wellcome Foundation. I know for instance that they have a map of Ireland showing where damage to children has happened. The map has colour-coded dots for deaths and various levels of damage. If I got my hands on that map, it would be in every newspaper.

Years later, the *Observer* newspaper in England revealed that the vaccine batch that had damaged Kenneth Best had also been used in the UK. They uncovered evidence that a boy in Wales had died after being injected with it, but that his parents had never been informed. Wellcome stated that they had no way of knowing exactly where and when the batch had been used in the UK, as there were no records of exactly which doctors in which areas had used the toxic vaccine.

The *Observer* uncovered the fact that there was also a second toxic batch released—3732—and that a further 14 batches were not tested at all. All batches were reported to contain 60,000 individual doses. In a typical response, a spokesman for GlaxoSmithKline, as it then was, told the *Observer:* "We do not accept that these batches were harmful." Business as usual—deny, deny, deny.

Ireland eventually brought in the safer acellular pertussis vaccine and had established a new set of procedures to try screening out babies who could be at risk of brain damage. But still no one here would give credence to the link with brain damage. The more public concern was raised, the more the medical professionals backtracked on the concerns they had been expressing among themselves for decades.

In fact, the whooping cough vaccine was known from the very beginning to be dangerous. The Danish research Madsen, in 1933, administered the vaccine to two babies and within hours both were dead. But in 1934, in the US alone, there were more than 265,000 cases of whooping cough, with 8,000 deaths. So the medical profession acknowledged the risks but persisted with the vaccine. It was only when the public became fully aware of the dangers that the medical profession and the pharmaceutical companies and governments started taking a different view. The new defence by experts became the view that the vaccine just happened to be administered at the same time that a problem the baby already had was first becoming apparent. It was a grand piece of double-think for separating cause and effect: if the baby is jabbed and falls sick then it's because the baby was going to fall sick anyway.

Time and again as we struggled for the truth, we were always told that the only way the vaccine could be accepted as the cause of the damage would be if we could prove our case in a court of law. But people don't realise how little access they have to medical information about themselves. Doctors and hospitals have the right to decide what documents will be shown to patients or even to the courts. It was the most aggravating block of all. As long as there was this denial of a link between the vaccine and the damage, and as long as there was all this contradictory evidence, and as long as there was this secrecy, the waters just kept getting muddier, and no one could make a concrete case that could set a precedent for all victims. There would be no more Margaret Bests in the Irish courts.

The political betrayals went on, too. In 1992, through another change in government, Dr John O'Connell was made Minister for

Health. This was the man who sat in our house in Coolock at the first meeting of the Association for Vaccine-Damaged Children. This was the man who had raised questions in the Dáil about the issue when it first came to light. This was the man who had sat by me and Charlie Haughey in the late 70s when we were facing then Minister for Health Brendan Corish. He had always been very sympathetic and a strong supporter of our cause. I wrote to him when he took office, saying, "I know you were very anxious to help me at that time and as you are in the right position maybe we can now get these families compensated." He wrote back saying the expert panel had done its job and the matter was closed.

The alarm had been raised. The controversy had ultimately caused changes that were saving babies from brain damage, and now we were all expected to go away and be quiet and get on with our lives. If we weren't going to do that, then evidence would be provided to show that what happened to our children was all just a coincidence. Time was on the government's side, too. Parents were getting older, their brain-damaged children were dying, Glaxo Wellcome stopped producing the vaccine, and the issue was so solidly bricked in by legal impossibilities that no one saw a way of proving the case of vaccine-damaged children. But my battle wasn't over. I still wanted justice for my Alan and I was a thorn in the government's side that was not going to go away.

Chapter 6 ∾

| ALAN

I lost Alan slowly. As the years went by, that dawned on me. Experts would talk of people with disabilities having a 'mental age' of whatever. But by the time Alan was 12 no one could say he had, for instance, a mental age of 2. Alan didn't have a mental age. From the time of the vaccinations he shrank back to being even more helpless than a baby, and meanwhile his body was racked and contorted by the convulsions. I was constantly battling to stop Alan from being pigeon-holed as severely mentally handicapped, and yet I was told once by a doctor who examined him that I was the problem: the doctor said I was an uncaring mother and wasn't giving Alan enough stimulation.

They were giving Alan drugs for the convulsions, but the drugs were almost knocking him out. I felt the medics had Alan nearly poisoned with drugs. It was either a matter of letting him go into a convulsion, or keeping him so sedated he was lifeless. When he was sedated, the fits still happened, but they were shorter. No amount of medication got rid of the fits. As Alan got older the convulsions became more severe and more frequent and they lasted longer. So Alan would be given more drugs, and on the cycle went. There was never a day in Alan's life from the time of the third vaccination that he did not have convulsions.

Alan was described as an epileptic. Epilepsy is a terrible affliction, but it is a treatable condition and epilepsy won't leave you with massive brain damage. A cousin of mine is epileptic. He is a married man with children and he lives a normal life. His epilepsy is under control. With Alan, no medic could ever explain why the outcome was different. The drugs that helped epileptics did not help Alan, and as time went by his condition became worse and worse. It was further proof of the brain damage caused by the vaccine.

Taking care of Alan was a constant struggle. It was difficult to dress him, it was difficult to feed him, and it was almost impossible to cut his hair as he kept moving his head from side to side. He was always in nappies—he was doubly incontinent. I would do anything for Alan, but feeding him was the hardest part. I would hold his chin with one hand and spoon-feed him with the other hand. But it was difficult to keep his head still and so the food might miss his mouth. All the food had to be mashed to a pulp because he couldn't chew.

The convulsions were the biggest problem and, as Alan grew, the biggest danger. There were at least three occasions when he had a fit as I was carrying him upstairs to his bedroom and he and I fell down the stairs together. I used to lift Alan on my shoulder to carry him. Kevin would always tell me to phone the Squash Club across the road from where we lived. Friends there would be willing to come over and help me carry Alan. But I felt that Alan was my child and that I should be the one taking care of him.

I remember one time Alan had a severe convulsion on the stairs and I was there trying to hold him. But he was so bad that I started to slip and I was taking him with me, so I let go of him and tumbled down and bashed my nose off a wall. I broke my nose twice with Alan—the other time being when he had a convulsion as I was holding him and his head jerked and he smashed my nose. I eventually needed surgery on my nose because I couldn't breathe properly through one side.

Throughout all this, I was trying to get on with an ordinary life. I gave birth to our second son, Karl, in April 1983. He was a fine, healthy baby and, needless to say, he received no vaccinations.

My daughter Olga used to mimic Alan when she was a little

child. "Is he stupid?" she would ask. "He won't answer me."

"He's one of God's special children," I would say.

"But why is he so stupid?" She was a young child learning to talk and she was looking at Alan, twice her size, not able to talk. In the end, when Olga would mimic Alan, we had to see the funny side of it. If you didn't see the funny side you'd go insane.

———

From time to time Kevin and I would just have to take a holiday. Kevin's sisters Maureen, Brigid and Ethel would take Alan sometimes, but other times Barbara Stokes would arrange for Alan to be taken in to St Ultan's Hospital. Whenever I went away and left Alan behind in hospital, I knew that when I saw him next he would have lost weight and he would be in a bad condition. In some ways it was understandable. Alan was not a sick child in hospital to be made better; he was there to be minded. He needed the kind of time and care the nurses could not afford to give him.

Once, I came back from a holiday to find that Alan's hands were in a shocking condition—cracked and sore because he had a habit of sucking his fingers and so his hands would become wet and infected. He constantly dribbled and, whereas I kept a cloth on his neck, in the hospital they put a plastic child's bib on him and his neck would become scalded. No one else would give Alan the care I gave him. No one else had the love for him that I had. It terrified me to think a day might come when he would have to be put permanently into such care. I would prefer if he was with God than with people who could not take care of him the way I would.

A mother's love is unconditional. With Alan I gave that love and received nothing in return. It didn't matter. Usually with a child people make sacrifices but also receive great pleasure: they give and receive love. But after what happened to Alan, he could never give me a hug or tell me he loved me or be pleased to receive something. Giving is easier when you also get something back, but that couldn't happen with Alan. With him, you loved someone who could give nothing in return. That's hard, but it never changed my love for my son. It was a wish of mine since Alan's childhood that he would give me a look of recognition. Not since before the vaccinations had there been a time when my son would look at me and smile.

In 1986 I was pregnant again. Alan slept in the room beside our bedroom. During the night we would be woken by a horrible screech, and we knew Alan was in a convulsion so I would go in to him. When Alan was in a fit, all I could do was stand and watch and die inside. It was like sticking knives in me. There was no way I could bring him out of a fit. All I could do was be there with him and watch him in his agony until the attack stopped.

As the pregnancy continued I became more and more exhausted. I had young Olga and Karl and my teenage daughter Tracey, and I was taking care of Alan. By then Alan was 13 and, like his father, tall. During the day I tended to him. In the evening before Kevin came home, I would carry Alan up the stairs—afraid that Kevin would see how difficult it was for me to manage. When night came, I would go to bed and be woken again by Alan in a convulsion. So Kevin made a decision. In the later months of the pregnancy, Kevin would grab me by the arm and stop me from going into Alan's room when he had a fit.

"You can't stop it and I'm not letting you look at him," he said. Later Kevin went further and moved Alan to a downstairs room to sleep at night, so that I might get a decent night's sleep.

In March 1987 I went into hospital and gave birth to our third son, and we named him Kevin after his father. The day before I was due to go home with our new baby, Kevin sat down alone with me in the hospital to break some shocking news.

"Alan will live in St Michael's House from now on," he said.

I wouldn't hear of it. "You can't lift him any more, Vera. It's all too much for you."

"I told you I'd put him in the ground once I couldn't lift him," I said.

Over time I had collected tablets that I kept in a jar in the highest press in the kitchen. I was always determined that when the day came when I couldn't take care of Alan, I would end his life. I'd languish in jail for the rest of my life as a result, but I had sworn to myself that my son was never going to be without my care.

"He's already gone to St Michael's," Kevin said.

I couldn't believe Kevin could do such a thing and I was hysterical. "Get him out of there!" I was crying.

Kevin begged me to listen to him. "You can't take care of him any more, Vera."

"When you collect me from here, we'll go and collect him from there so we can all go home together," I said.

My mother and my family came and implored me to accept what Kevin had done. "You can go up in the car any time to see him," my mother said, "but you can't do this any longer."

Eventually I accepted what everyone said. Alan was, after all, on Griffith Avenue—a short drive away from our home. But letting Alan go was the hardest thing I had ever done in my life. I have often wondered if I really would have ended Alan's life rather than see him taken away from me and put into care. I honestly think that I would have done so, regardless of the consequences. I felt that the little comfort he had in life was what I gave him, and without me he would have nothing more than a miserable existence. To love someone is to let them go. I was not willing to let Alan go to some institution, but I was willing to let him go to God.

———

I hated when Alan was in St Michael's. I was so angry at what had happened to him and I knew he should never have ended up in such a place. For two years I fought against the idea of his being there. All day long I would be thinking about him and whether or not they were taking proper care of him. I phoned them constantly, reminding them what way he liked his food and what food he liked.

In all the time Alan was in St Michael's, I never thanked the people there for their work. Instead, I was always watching to see if they made a mistake with him and I was always nit-picking. If I went up and they had a plastic bib on him, I would order them to take it off. I always wanted him to look as normal as possible. They had to give him the care I would give him. I said in my mind, the State has destroyed him, the medical system has covered it up, but now by God they'll give him the best care. It's the least they could do. I never walked out of there feeling grateful. Why would I? Kevin, being either kinder than me or less angry than me, would encourage me to be nice to the people there. He would say that what happened to Alan wasn't their fault. As far as I was concerned, it was their duty to give Alan the best possible treatment.

Once, I later learned that Alan had been placed too close to a radiator and his arm became jammed. He couldn't move himself. Unnoticed, he was left in agony and was burned. Another time a fellow patient knocked him over and he had to be taken to Temple Street Hospital for stitches. I was furious that I hadn't been contacted immediately when these things happened.

I also found out years later that Alan had often been taken out on visits by a woman who obviously was acting out of compassion. She would take him to her home for the day, but I was never told this at the time. My son was being brought to this woman's house and I knew nothing about her or about this arrangement. No matter how kind or considerate the woman might have been, my permission should have been sought before my son was placed in her care.

I would always go up to visit Alan without letting the hospital know I was going. I wanted to see if I could catch them not taking proper care of him. I would sneak in the back entrance. Not only did I want to check on how Alan was being treated, I also hated going in through the front entrance, where there was a communal room with some very extreme cases. I would see these people, and Alan would be there among them propped up in his wheelchair. I couldn't bear to see my son among such terrible cases of mental and physical retardation.

Alan had his own room, and I said he would be safer if he simply stayed in his room during the day. I would visit him and make sure above all that he was clean. I'd check his teeth and his hair and so on. Then I would try to get Alan on my lap, and I would sit there alone in the room with him. Sometimes I imagined that he knew I was holding him, but that was just wishful thinking. Indeed, I remember once arriving in Alan's room for a visit and there was a nurse in the room and she said, "Oh, he knows you're here. He's all excited."

"Do you realise what you're saying," I said. "That's my flesh and blood. If I thought for one second that he knew me, do you think I could walk away and leave him here? I know he doesn't know me. If he knew me I'd carry him on my back out of here. So don't ever say that again."

On each visit I'd go through all his clothes. There was a problem because not only was Alan growing, but the strong washes of the communal laundry would shrink his clothes. I would gather the clothes that no longer fitted him and put them all in a black sack. The staff wanted me to leave the clothes there—saying they would fit some of the other patients—but I never wanted to see Alan's clothes on anybody else. I would throw the sack in the boot of the car and drive down Griffith Avenue. There was a priest's house on my way home and I would stop the car, run up the path and leave the sack of clothes at his door.

I had worked in Arnott's department store for years, and I

would go in there to staff I knew and give them Alan's measurements. They would gather up a range of clothes for him. I didn't pick the clothes because I couldn't bear to. I couldn't look at a jumper, for instance, and think to myself, that'll look lovely on him. None of those pleasures a mother can have were possible for me.

Sometimes—as St Michael's was so near where we live—I would pass it by on my way to somewhere else. I would wonder how my son was and if I should pay him a visit. But I wouldn't be able to. I needed time to get myself prepared for a visit.

Kevin and I used to play cat and mouse. Kevin wouldn't tell me he had visited Alan, and I wouldn't tell him either. So a nurse might say to me, 'Oh his Dad was here yesterday', but Kevin would not have mentioned the visit to me. We were trying to protect one another from the hurt. There wasn't a time when I visited Alan that I didn't leave in tears, driving down Griffith Avenue roaring crying. Even when I got home I would still be crying, but when the time came that Kevin was due home, I would stop and clean myself up and put on a brave face. I'm sure Kevin did the same. He never came home to me distressed after visiting Alan.

After Alan was moved into full-time care in St Michael's, I asked people to stop sending me birthday cards for him. Receiving the cards just reminded me how bad his condition was. The older he became, the more profoundly obvious was the difference between him and teenagers his age. Every year was more hurtful, and with every year his condition worsened. The last photograph taken of him was when he was 17. He is lying almost naked on his bed, his frail body contorted by his suffering. It was taken as a record for legal reasons. After that, I saw no reason to have any more photographs of my poor son.

I never stopped fighting for justice for Alan. By 1995 Kevin and I were preparing a case to go to the High Court. As part of this process, we sought Alan's files from the Department of Health. They wrote back to our solicitors saying that all Alan's files were destroyed in a fire in 1989 and that the Edenmore Health Clinic had been demolished as a result of vandalism. By that time there were 15 cases of vaccine-damaged children that were preparing court actions. All were told that their files were lost or destroyed. It was, as journalist Sam Smyth described it, Catch 22. We wanted to take the government to court, but we wouldn't have a case without access to medical files and records in the possession of the government.

We simply couldn't believe that all our files had been lost by fire or whatever other accident. I wrote to the Minister for Health and pointed out what had happened. I had a letter dating from 1976 that stated all our files were "given the most careful and detailed consideration and evaluation". In my letter I asked:

1 By whom?
2 Their notes.
3 Copies of their reports.
4 What happened to the files when they were finished checking same?
5 Were copies made of the files? If so, where are they?

With regard to the letter stating that Alan's files had been destroyed in a fire in 1989—a letter in which it was also stated that there had been a history of vandalism at the Edenmore Health Clinic—I asked:

When were all of the break-ins at the Edenmore clinic? Please provide police reports. Who, if anybody, was ever charged?

Why were important files left unprotected? Who was responsible? Were they disciplined?

With regard to the fire in 1989: was anyone ever charged with causing the fire? Please show us the police report, fire department report, and Eastern Health Board report. Why were important files left unprotected knowing problems since 1967 as stated in your letter? How many files were destroyed? Have the various families been notified? Who gave the order to demolish the building? What measures were taken, if any, prior to the building being demolished to rescue files?

We were also told that extensive efforts were made in various locations to locate files on Alan—by whom? Where? When?

Is the Department of Health asking me to believe that with all the fuss we were creating since 1974 including meetings with your predecessors Mr Corish, Mr Haughey and Mr O'Connell that our files were lost/destroyed by fire?

I never received an answer to that letter.

I kept pushing our solicitors to set a date for getting into court, but they were still trying to gather evidence and supporting material.

"We have to get into court before he dies," I kept saying, and I think they didn't realise just how weak Alan was becoming. In time, the process of trying to get justice in court was starting to become meaningless. As the year was coming to a close, Alan's life was coming to an end.

Alan had become weaker and weaker. Towards the end, he was just skin covering bone. I remember putting my hand in under the sheet to touch him and feeling his bones through his skin. The bones were coming out of the sockets. He was wasting away. By then, Alan had become so frail that he could only lie on a water bed. His hips were dislocated, his ankles had collapsed, and one leg was permanently bent at the knee.

It was December 1995. Christmas was days away and all around there were people celebrating and being happy. I had long before learned to hate Christmas. I went up to visit Alan in St Michael's with new clothes. I found him gasping for breath in the bed. I said he was very sick, but the staff assured me that the doctor had examined him and that he had a very serious chest infection that was being treated. I knew he was very ill and I insisted that he be moved to a hospital, but they were sure there was no need. I went straight to a doctor friend at his clinic on the other side of town and told him how ill Alan was. He phoned the doctor dealing with Alan in St Michael's and was informed that Alan was on his way in an ambulance to the Mater Hospital. I drove straight away to the hospital. Alan was there in a trauma room and he was having terrible difficulty breathing. He had contracted pneumonia—a type that is very common in institutions and strikes the very frail.

I walked out of the room and a woman doctor said to me "That's the worst case of cerebral palsy I have ever seen."

"Oh no he's not," I said. "He has massive brain damage from the pertussis vaccine."

Immediately her defences were up.

"Who told you?" she said. "How do you know that?" It was the usual Irish response. She couldn't react with concern or with interest. She couldn't ask me to tell her what I thought. She had to put the wall up as I have seen again and again over the years. The Irish medical profession had never agreed there was a link between Alan's condition and the vaccine. And yet no doctor had ever explained to me what had happened to him. No one had ever put a name to whatever had caused his brain damage. All they ever did was deny, deny, deny.

Once when we were with Alan in the hospital, Kevin had gone out to have a smoke and was sitting on a bench in the grounds. As he was sitting there, he overheard a conversation between a group of doctors who were talking about Alan.

"Did you see Alan Duffy?" one said. "I've never seen such global brain damage from the pertussis vaccine."

"It's the worst case I've ever seen," another said. They were talking about Alan as if he were some kind of show case. When they were finished, Kevin went over to them.

"I'm Alan's Dad and I heard everything you said," he told them, and the colour drained from their faces.

Alan was moved to intensive care, and we knew it was the end for him. I remember once lifting him up and knowing he was thirsty. I tried to give him something to drink. He could hardly respond. There were nights when I held Alan and prayed to God to take him. Then I thought "I can't put another child of mine in the ground." It was selfish of me to want to hang on to him. As he became weaker, we were asked if we wanted him attached to an artificial respirator. He was becoming so weak he could not breathe. Soon, I couldn't even put my arms around him because there was so much equipment.

When Alan was dying, Kevin was my support. But nobody was helping Kevin. The poor man has always loved me to bits, and he was watching my every move. The night that Alan died, a wonderful thing happened. Alan turned his head and he had total recognition in his eyes. For the first time since he was a baby, he actually took in my whole face. It was as if, for one last moment, I had my child back. It was the first time I saw him at peace since he was a baby. Tracey was with me and she saw it too. She said afterwards that she even thought he was going to say something. I never saw Alan's eyes open after that.

On the night of 30 December 1995, Kevin and I had gone home to get some sleep. The doctors had said that Alan was as good as could be expected. In the middle of the night, 31 December, the phone rang. We were asked to come back into the hospital. We quickly dressed and went in. We walked down the corridor of the hospital and a nurse approached us as we reached the door of Alan's room. She told us he was dead. I went into the room. Not only was Alan dead, but all the medical equipment had been removed from around him at the bed. A candle was lighting beside his bed. I didn't understand. How long had he been dead before they called us? I found out afterwards that the time of Alan's death was recorded as 3.20 a.m. We had been phoned at 5 a.m. I realised then that when they had phoned us, they had already told Kevin that Alan was dead, but he didn't tell me. He carried the secret as we got dressed and went to the hospital.

In death, there was a look of relief on Alan's face. He looked like a normal tall and very handsome man. I actually felt relieved that Alan was dead. I felt he was out of his misery. He had spent almost all his life suffering, and that suffering was over. As I stood in the room, a priest came in. I refused to shake his hand.

I told Kevin I couldn't bear it if Alan was taken to the same funeral home used for Renee, and so he made sure to contact a different company. When I went to see Alan laid out in his coffin, the woman who had befriended him and taken him regularly to her home was there. I didn't want to be introduced to her. I knew she had been kind to him, but I was in a frame of mind where I felt she was a do-gooder who happened to choose Alan. I went to the coffin, looked at Alan and I thought he looked at peace. An uncle of mine, Emmet Dunne, was standing near me and told me the staff were about to close the coffin. I would never see my son again.

"He's not there," my uncle said to me. They were lovely words that helped me.

"No. He's not there—sure he's not?" I said.

Kevin and I were left alone in the room with the coffin, then the staff came and placed the lid. After that, there was the removal to the church for the funeral the following day.

When Alan died, Kevin said, "Do you know what we're going to do? We're going to take the funeral down to the Department of Health and we're going to hand in a letter of protest."

"Kevin," I said, "you'll turn his funeral into a circus."

"Well, it's been a circus all his life, Vera. We might as well finish it off with a grand finale."

"Okay," I said. "Let's do that."

We wrote a letter to the then Minister for Health, Michael Noonan:

> Dear Minister,
> This is to inform you that our son Alan died on 31 December 1995 from what we know to be complications as a direct result of the immunisation programme promoted by your department. We ask you now formally to admit the mistake of your department and to apologise unreservedly to our family.
> Yours Respectfully,
> Vera Duffy

Our family had contacted journalists and the Department of Health to let them know what we were about to do. As the funeral Mass was being held on 3 January 1996, journalists were gathered outside the church. As Kevin and I led the procession out of the church behind the coffin, I saw among the crowds the journalists, the television camera and the photographers and thought, this is when the circus begins.

The funeral cortège drove into the city and halted outside the offices of the Department of Health at Hawkins Street. The street was crowded with onlookers, supporters and journalists. Police were controlling the traffic. Kevin and I got out of our car, Alan's hearse in front of us, to walk up to the office building and hand in the letter. I remember Kevin saying to me, "Don't fall down, Vera. Hold your strength. Stay on your feet." He held on to me as we walked up to the door. The Minister wasn't there, or wouldn't come and face us. A secretary was there to accept our letter on his behalf.

I don't know how I managed that walk, but I collapsed in tears as I walked back towards the hearse. Kevin and our daughter Tracey held me up. I remember talking to a television journalist, but I don't remember what I said. Later, photographs of the incident were on the covers of all the national newspapers.

The cortège then carried on out to Sutton Cemetery. I was sobbing, and I remember someone in my family asking me to stop crying. "She has to cry," I heard someone else say. "Let her cry."

For the second time we were burying a child. Alan was buried with his sister Renee. She had died at the age of 3. His life had been stolen from him when he was five months old. I remember looking at the gravestone and seeing the words 'God works in mysterious ways'. I don't know who had chosen the inscription— maybe it was Kevin.

While Renee's funeral remains a complete blank to me, I remember Alan's very clearly. Maybe it was because I was so relieved as I knew his suffering was over. In the years since Renee died, I had only been to the grave once. I swore that day that I would never in my life go back to it again. I never have.

After the funeral we went to a nearby hotel for tea and sandwiches. A lot of the staff of St Michael's were there, and Kevin was encouraging me to be nice to them. But I didn't talk with them. I suppose I still felt strange—as if Alan had been half mine and half theirs.

Again, it was all over the papers. Again, there were calls by the politicians who were *not* in power to do something about this terrible situation. Willie O'Dea, the Fianna Fáil TD and opposition spokesman for law reform, said there should be a no-fault compensation scheme set up for vaccine-damaged children. Michael Noonan, the Minister for Health, replied to our letter, saying:

> I realise the depth of the anguish which you have felt throughout the years, and that this might in some way be eased if it was possible for the Department to make the admission which you have requested. I very much regret that it is not possible to do this, since a link between Alan's condition and the immunisation which he received is not

established by the medical records which are available to the Department and which have been supplied in the past to you and your solicitor.

A Department of Health spokesman told reporters that the Department was co-operating fully with us. This enraged Kevin who pointed out to a reporter that these same people had told us six weeks previously that Alan's files had been destroyed, yet could not give us specific dates for when this had happened. Nor could they explain what happened to copies of those files sent to Ministers for Health down through the years of our battle, or copies sent from one hospital to another. We were burying Alan and I'm sure the Department of Health thought they were burying us.

A long time later, I got Alan's medical file from his years in care. I was still looking for evidence to prove what had happened to him. I knew reading the file would break my heart, but I swore I would do it once. What I read made me sorry that I hadn't ended his life earlier. I believe that Alan could feel pain, and he must have been in terrible pain. In later years he had to have daily enemas. Towards the end of his life they had to put him on a waterbed in an effort to give him some relief from pain because his limbs were becoming dislocated. He had fits almost daily.

When I was reading the file, I came upon some ridiculous reports that were being made about Alan—saying he had 'gone bowling' or that he was being considered for the Special Olympics. Furious, I phoned up St Michael's demanding to speak to the man in charge. In my anger I obviously sounded like I had some authority, because the secretary I spoke to gave me the man's mobile phone number. I rang the mobile and all he wanted to know was how I got his number. I told him I had been going through Alan's file and that I wanted a letter stating that abilities Alan was credited with were not possible.

"Like what?" he asked.

I listed the things written—that Alan enjoyed swimming and bowling, was being considered for the Special Olympics and that he liked to make his own decisions.

"If that's what was written, then that's the truth," was the reply.

Later, the same man wanted me to go and talk with him about the report. I made an appointment and never showed up. He then wrote to me saying that the file was legal and could not be altered. So yes, Kevin was more considerate and kind in dealing with these people. But I found time and time again that their first concern was always to cover for each other. Why should I be grateful or be nice with them? The comments were probably written by volunteers or workers who were ashamed to leave report pages blank, so they made up things about his 'communication skills' and 'recreation' that left the impression that Alan had something that had been stolen from him—a life.

Going through Alan's medical records, I found a total of 10 different references to his condition being the result of brain damage caused by the vaccine. All those specifics are listed in the chapter written by Martin Duffy at the end of this book.

———

All over the world, people have acknowledged and addressed the dangers of vaccination. Not in Ireland. In Ireland they never gave credence to all the evidence. The government just wanted the subject—and me—to go away. When poor Alan died, I imagine they all breathed a sigh of relief. For me it was the reverse. When Alan died I thought, now he's dead, I won't have to worry about him and I'll take you bastards on. I was no longer holding back for fear Alan wouldn't be taken care of. Nothing could hold me back.

The new battleground soon became clear when I got a phone call from someone in the Mater Hospital saying that the cause of death on Alan's death certificate would be 'aspirational pneumonia as a result of cerebral palsy'.

"Over my dead body," was my response. "Now my son is dead and we can all play games."

I swore I would not accept a death certificate for my son that did not place the blame for his death directly on the vaccine. And I was ready to give everything in that battle. People have often asked me how I have remained so angry for so many years. The injustice done to my son, to my family and to me has kept the fire burning in me. As long as the system denied the truth and blocked me, I was going to keep on fighting. In my next battle, I found a man who was my least likely ally: the Dublin City Coroner.

Chapter 7 ∾

| JUSTICE

They couldn't say they were sorry. They were afraid to, because accepting blame opened the door to facing the consequences. And yet that's all I wanted: not their money, not anyone's job, not any company's reputation, just an admission that mistakes were made and would not be made again. It would have given some small sense of purpose to Alan's life of suffering. But no, they fought me every step of the way and were sure they would wear me down until I went away. My anger kept me going. I would not give in.

After Alan died, my solicitor advised me to abandon the planned court case because, even if we won, the compensation we might receive would not come close to the huge costs of a court case. Before I raised the alarm about the dangers of vaccination, medical experts in Ireland were saying the risk should be accepted and provisions made for it. But they wanted it on their own terms. When too many people knew about the risks, the same experts built walls around the truth.

The terrible thing about the attitude of the State and the medical profession is that they throw it back at you. They say, 'prove it'. The evidence gathered over the years is not enough to bring an apology and an acknowledgment. They still say, prove it, and then do all they can to prevent you from doing so. So when some ordinary person goes to a solicitor to take up the case, the advice is that the cost of the case could run into millions and the solicitor can't afford to take the risk of supporting it. The State and the pharmaceutical companies are going to bring in the best they can get. They have unlimited funds and are going to fight you with all the might they can muster. The pharmaceutical companies had thrived on the vaccines that had destroyed Alan, and the government could not afford to pay the price of their vaccination policy, so no expense would be spared to shut up people like me.

There was still one last possibility for me—one last chance to see justice done for Alan. I put together a file of information about Alan and went to the offices of the Dublin City Coroner. I sat in a chair in the reception area of the court. Brian Hanney, the manager of the Coroner's Office, came out to me. I told him I was not leaving until I had seen the coroner.

"You have to make an appointment," Brian said.

"I'm not making an appointment," I said. "I want to meet him. I want him to see me."

I handed Brian the file and he went away. Time passed. Then the coroner, Brian Farrell, came out to me holding the file and introduced himself. He told me that any case he considered had to be brought to him by a medical person. "I can't agree to an inquest that you ask for," he explained.

Suggesting to me at that stage that I should go to a medical person for help showed just how little Brian knew about my battle. But I would not be put off so easily. Dr MacMathuna was the man who had admitted Alan into the Mater Hospital. I made an appointment and went to see him along with my daughters Olga and Tracey. I sat down with my daughters either side of me and I said: "Now you are going to hear what happened to my son."

I told him the story of the vaccination and of all the lies I had been told since then. I told him I wanted a proper hearing. When the doctor heard my story, he agreed to my request. He said he would write to Brian Farrell seeking an inquest into the cause of Alan's death. Kevin and I waited, and we were contacted by Brian Farrell for a meeting. We talked through Alan's story with him and he said he would be in contact with his decision. Farrell considered the evidence and the case, and then contacted Dr MacMathuna with his decision: he would hold an inquest into the cause of Alan's death.

As the coroner was preparing for the inquest, I was becoming more friendly with his assistant, Brian Hanney. I told him straight out that I didn't trust him. "How could I trust you? You work for the State." I told Brian that I didn't believe that the Irish government, or the medical profession, would let the coroner declare the true cause of Alan's death. Brian Farrell contacted me and assured me that he was totally independent from any outside influence. "I answer to nobody," he said. "It is my function to get to the truth."

"They won't let you," I told him.

"They can't stop me," he said.

"You mark my words," I said. "They'll stop you."

Brian Farrell didn't believe me. "I'm the coroner. No one would stop my work."

It took months for me to start trusting Brian Farrell. I was going to the offices regularly, bringing more documentation and finding out what was happening. As my trust in Farrell grew, his understanding of what he was facing also began to become clearer.

In the 1970s, before Renee died, I had been trying to prepare a case that could go to court. That never happened. Before Alan's death, we had been preparing to go to the High Court. We abandoned that when Alan died. There could no longer be a case seeking compensation, but I had a chance through the coroner's inquest to have the truth told. By the time the inquest was being prepared, I was far more informed and I had far more connections. I was ready to bring in experts from all over the world. And I was ready to remortgage the house to fund my case. I had set my sights on getting justice for Alan. I think at that stage, too, the Department of Health was not going to do anything to obviously block my way. I was a grieving mother and they would let me have my day in court. I wanted to take advantage of that opportunity.

The topic of vaccination was not going away from the public eye. While the coroner was gathering research and information for Alan's inquest, new scandals about vaccination were coming to light. All the disgraceful events came as a result of one simple fact: up to 1987 there was no legislation governing drug trials in Ireland. So in the 60s and 70s drug trials were carried out here without the knowledge or consent of the parents or guardians of babies. Later it was pointed out that these experiments by their very nature even contravened the Nuremberg Code, a 1947 judgement made by the War Crimes Tribunal following Nazi atrocities:

The voluntary consent of the human subject is absolutely essential. This means that the person involved should have legal capacity to give consent, should be situated as to be able to exercise free power of choice, without the intervention of any element of force, fraud, deceit, duress, overreaching or other ulterior form of constraint or coercion; and should have sufficient knowledge and comprehension of the elements of the subject matter involved as to enable him to make an understanding and enlightened decision. This latter element requires that before the acceptance of an affirmative decision made by the experimental subject, there should be made known to him the nature, duration and purpose of the experiment; the method and means by which it is to be conducted; all hazards and inconveniences reasonably to be expected; and the effect upon his health of person which may possibly come from his participation in the experiment. The duty and responsibility for ascertaining the quality of the consent rests upon each individual who initiates, directs or engages in the experiment. It is a personal duty and responsibility which may not be delegated to another with impunity.

The first wave of the scandals broke when it was revealed that Prof. Irene Hillary, working on behalf of the Wellcome Research Laboratory, had carried out three research trials in orphanages and 'in the wider community' from the early 60s to the mid-70s. It was later discovered that children with disabilities had been included in the trials. Dr Victoria Coffey is a retired paediatrician who had helped with the trial at the children's home where she worked. Her comment to the *Irish Independent* newspaper when the story broke was: 'Many people put their children into the home because of convenience. People just relinquished their responsibility but now they are fussing about this.'

Prof. Hillary stated that she was 'extremely concerned by the irresponsible reporting by the media' and that 'these children would have been vaccinated at or about the same time by the medical officers at the homes . . .'

Wellcome, in their official statement, said: 'Wellcome conducted its studies in accordance with accepted medical and ethical standards of the time . . . For necessary reasons of medical and legal confidentiality, it is not appropriate for Glaxo Wellcome to comment publicly on individual patients.' In other words—and as usual—no one was apologising.

The controversy brought the old battles to the front pages once again. Prof. Hillary was quoted as saying she did not believe Kenneth Best's condition was caused by the vaccine. The retired chief medical officer of the Eastern Health Board, Brendan O'Donnell, who had chaired the expert panel that we wouldn't support in the late 70s, said the panel had been too lenient. "We found only 14 children out of over a hundred may have been damaged," he said. This is the kind of language parents like me were confronted with: 'only 14 children'. Mister One-in-a-Million hadn't lost his touch when it came to concern for public welfare.

One trial—the results of which were never published—compared the effects of the standard DPT vaccine and a newer, cheaper one being developed. It was done in 1973—the year Alan was destroyed—and 53 children in orphanages and 65 children living at home in the Dublin area were the innocent human guinea pigs. A Wellcome memo said that Prof. Hillary was researching 'allegations of serious adverse reactions to DPT vaccine in Ireland'.

In August to October 1973 there was a set of correspondence between the Eastern Health Board and Wellcome about a high number of bad reactions to the DPT vaccine. Margaret Dunlevy, deputy Chief Medical Officer, reported to Dr A.H. Griffith, head of the Department of Clinical Immunology at Wellcome, that there were adverse reactions, particularly from certain batches. She reported 70 children with reactions—40 with temperatures of 105–106 degrees—in the previous few months. 'These frequent reactions are causing us concern as regards the advisability of continuing Trivax', she wrote on 22 August 1973. A week later, to answer queries from Wellcome, she explained: 'It is the usual practice that our Immunisation Officer visits the homes when reactions are notified but occasionally the General Practitioner may be called out, much to their annoyance. Four of these reaction cases were admitted to hospital due to hyperpyrexia.' She sent copies of reports on two babies who had experienced infantile spasms. She added: 'We have some material of Batches 84657, 84018, 84019 which we used in Dr Hillary's survey.'

In September 1973, Dunlevy wrote to Wellcome and she expressed a view about what the vaccinated children were suffering that to her was plainly matter-of-fact but for any parent is chilling to read: 'We are not so much worried about these from a clinical aspect but they cause considerable damage to the immunisation scheme. Our nurses report that mothers are reluctant and often refuse further immunisation when a child has reacted badly. We attempt to cover 80% of the child population but we fear that may be difficult to continue.' In that letter she also wrote—and this from the deputy Chief Medical Officer of an organisation which has been denying any link between the pertussis vaccine and brain damage—seeking 'the possibility of reducing or altering the pertussis element in the vaccine'.

But the real bombshell was yet to land. Brian McDonald of the *Irish Independent* came up with an amazing discovery. During the trials being referred to in the correspondence above, batch numbers were being listed. Incredibly, Wellcome ran the same set of serial numbers for human and animal vaccines, and batches of the animal vaccine Tribovax T had been sent to Ireland along with batches of the DPT vaccine Trivax. Irish babies had been injected with a cow vaccine for blackleg, braxy, black disease, bacterial redwater and tetanus. Not only that, but one of the batches of this cow vaccine was being used in Prof. Hillary's research.

According to Wellcome documents, there are 60,000 doses in a batch. The Tribovax T batches shown to have been used here included numbers 84496, 84769, 84795 and 84796. Batch numbers mentioned to be in use in Hillary's experiments were 84657, 84018 and 84019. Batch numbers the Eastern Health Board were expressing concerns about in August 1973 (two months before Alan's first injection) were 84008, 84018, 84019, 84657 and 84769. The batch numbers used on Alan were 85274, 85401 and 85404. In September 1969, Kenneth Best was injected with toxic vaccine from batch number 3741. How quick did they go through batch numbers? How separate was the manufacture of one batch from another?

More truth kept coming out. Wellcome had admitted to trials being carried out in Ireland up to 1973, but there were references to tests being carried out up to 1976. There also seemed to have been two research trials in 1973, though at first only one was being admitted. Then, in its own official statement explaining how the mix-up with the cow vaccine might have happened, Wellcome inadvertently listed another cow vaccine batch as a human batch that had been sent to Ireland at the time. The adults who had been children in these orphanages were also discovering that they had no right to access information about what they had been injected with, and would have to take a court order against Wellcome to find out the truth. There were calls for a public inquiry, and the then Health Minister Brian Cowen ordered a report.

It was as all this documentation was being made public that I found something very relevant to Alan and quoted earlier in this book. It was standard procedure for the Eastern Health Board to issue a sheet stating 'Immunisation Procedure' to the health clinics. Under the section about the DPT vaccine, the January 1974 sheet that was addressed to 'Each immunisation doctor and all members of the immunisation staff', had a new paragraph warning: 'If you learn that after a previous injection the child was unnaturally limp or drowsy, or had a convulsion or any other sign of Encephalopathy, a further injection must not be given. . . .' That had been sent out a month before my Alan was given his third injection. It had been stated policy at the time Neil O'Doherty first examined Alan and expressed concerns about his being limp and having a problem 'of obscure origin'. I'd had to wait decades to see that in black and white in my hands.

Shocking as all these revelations were, the topic of vaccine trials on Irish babies being used as the guinea pigs of a British drugs company had not yet been fully told. There was worse yet to be uncovered.

———

The coroner had gathered all his material. The Eastern Health Board was co-operating by giving any documentation requested. Mind you, all medical files were first being checked by all concerned and all had the right to withhold any document they wanted. So what did Brian Farrell actually get?

There was another fine irony. Prof. Neil O'Doherty, who had first identified a problem 'of obscure origin' with Alan between the second and third vaccines and with whom Kevin and I had had so many problems over the years, was approached by the Coroner's Office to give details of the case. He was, by then, retired. He wrote back to the coroner saying: "This is to confirm, as stated in my earlier letter of 20th May 1997, that I was never in contact with Alan Duffy, deceased, and I will therefore not be able to help you in your post-mortem proceedings."

By the time the inquest began, I was starting to believe I would finally get answers to my questions about what had happened to my son. Times had changed: people no longer had the old slavish mentality towards doctors (or the other broken pillars—the Church and the State); journalists had been revealing all kinds of secrets regarding the vaccination programme, and there seemed to be a real chance to have the truth acknowledged. I also felt that, since there was no longer any question of suing on behalf of Alan or seeking compensation, the focus could be on finding the truth and on nothing else. Matters of civil or criminal liability cannot be considered by the coroner. The inquest would also take place before a jury. I believe this was due to the fact that the cause of Alan's death would fall under the heading in the Coroner's Act 1962: "that the death of the deceased occurred in circumstances the continuance or possible recurrence of which would be prejudicial to the health or safety of the public or any section of the public".

The inquest began on Thursday 4 December 1997. There were reports prepared by medical experts, and some medical correspondence from the Eastern Health Board. The inquest started off in a very polite and simple way. Dr MacMathuna said he would describe aspirational pneumonia as the cause of death, but said that this had been a result of Alan's neurological condition.

I gave evidence about the time when Alan had his vaccinations, and I showed photographs of Alan, happy and healthy, in his early months. I had been determined to stay calm as I gave evidence, but I broke down when I said: "Like all young mothers, all I wanted was what was best for my baby." A medical professional I cannot name for legal reasons said of the photographs of Alan smiling, 'but that's just a posed picture' and claimed I had told him Alan had always been an odd child who had never smiled.

Niall O'Donohoe, the neurologist who had treated Alan as a child and many years beyond that, said there had been some fears in the 70s of a link between the pertussis vaccine and brain damage, but these had since been dismissed. He said that even in instances where babies had febrile seizures after vaccinations, these symptoms would go away unless the baby was coincidentally suffering from a condition that was just then manifesting.

Dr Stokes and Prof. Tempany also gave their evidence, talking about Alan's diagnosis and treatment over the years.

John Wilson, the London specialist who had first diagnosed a link between Alan's condition and the vaccine, gave a report on the case. He summarised by saying: 'It is my opinion that there is strong prima facie evidence indicating that Alan Duffy did suffer adverse reactions to triple vaccine, reactions to which he was disposed by virtue of having an intrinsically progressive/degenerative neurological illness which had not yet declared itself at the time of the first injection.' Wilson had changed his view from the original diagnosis and at first I was angry about that. It took me a while before I could come around to accepting that even if Wilson was right—that my son had epilepsy, for instance—the extreme damage was triggered by the vaccine. But I was disappointed in him.

A report supplied by Prof. Peter Behan of the Department of Neurology, University of Glasgow, which also referred back to an international medical workshop in the US, concluded: 'The data given in this report in my opinion strongly supports the concept that post-pertussis vaccination encephalopathy is a genuine neurological entity.' Behan also stated of Alan's case: 'It is clear that because of the temporal profile, the infantile spasms and the resultant encephalopathy, in my opinion, are secondary to that immunisation. What is also important is that the second immunisation should not have been given, there being strong contra-indications to the second and third immunisations.'

Behan elsewhere quoted research into the vaccine: 'The incidence of convulsions after pertussis vaccination was 1 in 2,200 vaccinated, there being 1 case of permanent damage among 20,600 children vaccinated. There were 73,445 cases that were immunised with diphtheria tetanus vaccine in which only 1 seizure was reported.'

A report supplied by Prof. John Stephenson took the opposite view. Stephenson was the man who, in the High Court case many years before, had provided the medical view that Daragh Murphy had not been vaccine damaged. His report was a highly academic paper that concluded, like O'Donohoe's, that what people thought were reactions were instead the coincidental early onset of epilepsy. Meaning, as far as I am concerned, blame it on coincidence. 'I pushed him and he fell, but he was already losing his balance.'

The senior counsel for the Eastern Health Board was Michael McDowell—later Minister for Justice. He was very gentle and very nice at the outset, but became more and more concerned at the way in which he felt the inquest was trying to attribute blame for Alan's death. At later sessions the Health Board wanted to halt the inquest. The judge pointed out that if they had agreed to take part they could not pull out simply on the basis that they were not pleased with how things were going. With all the time I spent with or around Brian Farrell and his co-workers, I believe I noticed a little peculiarity in this always smartly-dressed man: when he felt under pressure and was in a bad mood, he wore a dicky bow instead of an ordinary tie.

There were days when I would say to Kevin, 'I cannot face any more of this disgusting circus.' I would look at the people representing the State and think, if this happened to their child, would they understand how I am feeling? But it was not their child, and anyway it was probably a well-paid job to them. I could not put a figure on what this did to us financially and emotionally. Every time I left the court the press were there. I got sick of seeing myself in tears in newspapers. Then I would go home and look at all this documentation from the pharmaceutical companies and think, my God, how many did this kill or destroy? At one stage, back when I had formed the Irish Association for Vaccine-Damaged Children, I knew of 370 victims. Where had they all gone? Alan was dead. How many of them were also dead or in institutions? Was I the last chance for those lost children to get justice?

With all this complicated evidence and conflicting views, Farrell decided to commission a report from an independent medical expert. He adjourned the inquest until this report was completed. The person the coroner chose to draw up the report was Dr Karina Butler, an infectious diseases consultant to Temple Street Hospital, Our Lady's Hospital in Crumlin and the Eastern Health Board. Around the time of Alan's death, she had been interviewed in the *Sunday Tribune* and had warned of an epidemic if children were not vaccinated against whooping cough. Needless to say, I did not hold out high hopes for the conclusions she would reach in her report.

It was a year and a half before the inquest sat again. The report Dr Butler produced was 43 pages long and gave an overview of all the different ways research was being interpreted. It came to a very weak conclusion: 'No consistent, unique, clinical entity recognisable as pertussis vaccine encephalopathy has emerged . . . Neither has the possibility that such events might very rarely occur been conclusively excluded.' The report also said that 'an association between DPT administration and first febrile seizure has been noted', but again stated that this was 'temporal'—it just happened to occur at the same time. The report obviously wasn't of any help to my case regarding the cause of Alan's death. There was a session of the Coroner's Court in February 1999 to consider the delivery of the report, and then Brian Farrell decided to adjourn until 19 April for a three-day session to conclude the case.

By then, however, the Eastern Health Board had had enough. They wrote to Farrell through their solicitors telling him that no clear link between the vaccine and brain damage had been proven and it was time he issued a verdict of pneumonia as the cause of death. They listed sections of the 1962 Coroner's Act, defining the role of the coroner, and said he was going beyond what a coroner was allowed to do. They said he was going into areas that might indicate criminal or civil liability and the Act did not allow that. They said he was allowed only to identify the person who is the subject of the inquest and to establish 'how, when and where' the death occurred. The Eastern Health Board wanted the coroner to do things their way and keep away from their vaccination programme.

Farrell informed the Eastern Health Board solicitors that he was proceeding with the inquest dates in April. They then pressed for a judicial review. The Eastern Health Board went to the High Court to halt Alan's inquest. They were pulling no punches. They said that the coroner was acting 'ultra vires'—beyond the limits of the 1962 Coroner's Act. They claimed that the 16-month delay waiting for the Butler report was excessive. They claimed also that the coroner was restricted by law from carrying out a general inquiry into the whole cell pertussis vaccine in relation to Alan's death. They wanted an order of Mandamus to compel the coroner to deliver a verdict of 'aspirational pneumonia' as the cause of Alan's death without qualification. They wanted a declaration that the coroner had acted in an unreasonable and unfair manner. They wanted a declaration that it was unnecessary for the coroner to hold an inquest into Alan's death. The gloves were off and sympathy for the grieving mother had run out. I was seeing again what I had warned Brian Farrell of at the outset. In my heart, I always knew that somehow or other he would be prevented from reaching the truth, just as I had been. The system would stop at nothing to preserve and protect itself.

In November 1999, the coroner and the Eastern Health Board faced Mister Justice Geoghegan as Kevin and I, as Notice Parties, sat with our legal representative Paul Gardiner. Brian Farrell denied any breach of his jurisdiction, and Paul Gardiner accused the EHB of being patronising in the way they wanted to control, and not trust, the jury. The judge heard all the arguments and at the end he reserved judgement, needing time to weigh up all that had been presented to him.

In his judgement a month later, Mister Justice Geoghegan decided:

> If the Eastern Health Board is correct in its legal arguments it is wholly against the public interest that the inquest should be allowed to continue in the manner in which it has been carried out. There is power under the Coroner's Act for a jury to make a recommendation and the Health Board makes no secret of the fact that it is afraid that a misguided jury could make a recommendation not warranted on the evidence but which could be extremely damaging to public confidence in the vaccine practices.

Citing previous cases from Ireland and the UK, the judge stated: "What the coroner was concerned with was the proximate medical cause of death." The judge upheld the objection of the Eastern Health Board. I sat there listening to the judge, then I just got up and walked out. I knew the wall was up again. I knew that the Health Board had yet again found a way to stop me from reaching the truth.

When we lost in the High Court, Brian Farrell wanted to

pursue the matter to the Supreme Court. But he was working for the government, and why would his employers fund him to take on the Eastern Health Board—another one of their own departments. The Department of Health, through the Department of Justice, refused to fund the coroner to take the matter to the Supreme Court. It seemed like the end of the line.

"They think I'm going to stop now," he said, "but I'm going into my own personal funds."

"I haven't got that kind of money to underwrite you," I said, "but I'll do the best I can."

"No, you won't," he said. "I'm doing this."

Never in the history of the State had this happened. The coroner was taking a case against the government to the Supreme Court. Brian Farrell was showing a courage I hadn't come across before. It was the first time someone in a position of real authority in Ireland had stood by me. I had seen plenty of politicians give support for what I was doing when it helped them get votes, then abandon me when they came into power, but this man had made a commitment to finding out the truth about Alan and he was sticking to his word.

So began another battle in my endless war.

Chapter 8 ∾

| LONG BATTLES

I had been locked in battle in Ireland for so long that it was a great boost to my morale to discover the National Vaccine Information Center in Virginia, US. The people who set it up have won their war: they have succeeded in establishing in the US the kind of fair and open solution I wish existed in Ireland. People in America have done what we have failed to do in Ireland: make the pharmaceutical companies and the government answerable for the casualties of the immunisation programme.

Vaccination is mandatory in the US. A child will not be allowed into school unless he or she has been vaccinated. Even if one of your children had a bad reaction, they would still insist on vaccinating your other children. The medical profession there is so fixed on vaccinating that they will inject a child who might be in hospital for some other reason. Children have been vaccinated when they accompanied another child to a hospital or a doctor's clinic. So extreme is the push for vaccination that the National Vaccine Information Center has warned parents not to sign any documents presented to them *during childbirth* because some couples found out later they had signed over the right to have their baby injected.

The National Vaccine Information Center was set up by Kathi Williams and Barbara Loe Fisher. Kathi told me that she saw an article about me and Alan and the story raised her suspicions about what had happened to her own son. Barbara also had a child damaged by vaccine. These two women got together and decided to look more into what was happening in the US. In 1981 they started by having what they called 'angels parties'—where they sought funds to develop the organisation. They started getting media coverage and were raising public awareness. When they appeared on television, the letters started pouring in. Kathi and Barbara were uncovering the true extent of the problem of vaccine-damaged children in the us.

The campaign I started in Ireland in the mid-70s was nothing compared to how the American parents reacted when they learned the truth. As momentum gathered, the people marched on Congress to force the government into a decision.

There were congressional hearings and Congressman Dan Burton became a hero of the cause. Dan, who became chairman of the Government Reform Committee looking into the links between vaccination and autism, had seen the dangers of the vaccination programme at first hand. His granddaughter Alexandra, at the age of six weeks, received her second Hepatitis vaccination and stopped breathing. She spent two weeks in hospital and a year on a breathing monitor before she fully recovered. His grandson Christian was a healthy, outgoing, talkative 14-month old when his mother took him for a vaccination appointment. At that one visit, in a routine procedure, the child was given nine vaccinations. He was never the same again. That night he was emitting high-pitched screams. He began dragging his head on the furniture and banging it repeatedly. Within a week and a half he could no longer speak. He no longer made eye contact. He disappeared into the world of autism and never recovered. As Dan Burton said: "My only grandson became autistic right before my eyes shortly after receiving his federally recommended and state-mandated vaccines."

In 1986 Congress passed the National Childhood Vaccine Injury Act, which set up a system for compensating families of vaccine-injured children. One of the Bill's main supporters was Senator Ted Kennedy. His nephew, Robert F. Kennedy Jun., is also very active in the field and has written about the dangers of vaccines. While I had caught different experts saying the pertussis vaccine was or was not dangerous for some babies, research in the US showed that the main suspect there for the damage being caused is the substance Thimersol, which is a mercury-based preservative used to supply the vaccine in bulk and thereby save costs. Research continued on the pertussis vaccine in the US, however, and this is a quote from the National Vaccine Information Center:

> In 1994 another special committee of experts at the Institute of Medicine took a second look at the association between DPT vaccine and permanent brain damage. They reviewed the conclusions of a Ten Year Follow-up of the landmark British National Childhood Encephalopathy Study, published in 1981 . . . the IOM committee concluded that 'some children who receive DPT and who experience a serious acute neurological illness within seven days thereafter should be expected to go on to experience chronic nervous system dysfunction or die.'

As the controversy grew, the drug companies went to the government and said they would stop making drugs for the vaccination programme if they were going to be at risk from huge law suits. The solution reached was to put a tax on the vaccines, and that money was put into a pool that formed a compensation fund for children damaged by the United States' vaccine programme. A panel of experts was established and parents could put their case to this panel who would investigate the case and rule on it. This would not stop the parents from taking a case to court, but this was an easier—possibly more civilised—route. Rates were set with a 'price' for death and different levels of damage. That system was established in 1987.

By the end of 1996, the federal vaccine compensation programme created by the National Childhood Vaccine Injury

Act had made awards to nearly 1,000 vaccine victims and the majority of these awards were made for injuries or deaths caused by the DPT vaccine. The awards totalled nearly $750 million. But as time went by, the NVIC started questioning the wisdom of government policy. It wasn't enough to have compensation in place. Surely this loss or destruction of life was wrong. Most of the medical profession in the US were still in favour of vaccination, and even though there were strict procedures about who might not safely be vaccinated, or what the contra-indications were, there was continued pressure on parents to vaccinate their children.

The National Vaccine Information Center is dedicated to helping parents make informed decisions about vaccinating their children. In 1987, Barbara Loe Fisher and H.L. Coulter co-wrote a book called *A Shot in the Dark* about the possible dangers of vaccination. Like me, Barbara and the people at NVIC are not against vaccination; they are against ignorance. Their work is about helping parents—and, indeed, doctors—make informed decisions. This quote from Barbara in the NVIC literature is very powerful:

> Parents in every country of the world continue to take healthy, bright children of all ages to paediatric offices and public health clinics to get vaccinated and then tragically watch their children die or be left brain-damaged. After a child has died or been injured by a vaccine or a combination of vaccinations almost always government health officials deny and cover up what really happened. They are more anxious to reassure the public with a lie than to honestly acknowledge the truth about vaccine risks and take action to minimize them. It is no wonder that parents have become mistrustful of those operating a mass vaccination system more concerned about protecting the status quo than protecting the lives of innocent children who have no voice and often have no choice.

My main interest, because of Alan, was to learn more about the pertussis vaccine. All I have learned shows me that it is a terrible vaccine with a shocking history. In the US three and a half million children are given their first DPT shot every year, and one in seven have such contra-indications that they are given no more pertussis vaccine in the following injections. One study in the US said: '1 in 875 DPT shots results in a convulsion or a collapse/shock reaction.' But in the same study, two babies died and were classified as cot deaths with no connection to the vaccine. If that were not bad enough, statistics show that half the cases of pertussis happen to children who have been vaccinated.

The pertussis vaccine was first used in the US in 1936 and has been in general use since the early 40s. Statistics show that diseases like diphtheria, polio, whooping cough and so on, were already in steep decline before the introduction of vaccines. Why? Because the general nutrition and welfare of people was improving and healthier babies were not as prone as undernourished children.

I don't know what the balance is between the dangers of the illness and of the vaccination. It's clear that the majority of babies who get the vaccination are at least not harmed by it, whatever about whether they are helped by it. But if someone gave me the choice between nursing my child through the whooping cough—'the hundred day cough', as some call it—and risking brain damage, I would of course choose three months of caring for him over the loss of his life.

But other vaccines have been linked to other damage in infants. The MMR—measles, mumps, rubella—vaccine is suspected of links to brain damage. The Salk vaccine for polio—the one that I and my generation was given in school—is believed to have initially caused an increase in polio. In 1977 the man who invented the vaccine, John Salk, said most if not all cases of polio since the 60s were being caused by the vaccine itself.

And the very notion of mass immunisation is questioned by

those who say it is a biological time bomb. A lot of the ingredients in vaccines are actually poisons, including mercury, formaldehyde and aluminium. Meanwhile, vaccines are prepared through, or contain, such things as monkey kidney, calf serum and chick embryo. In the US, a child will have 37 vaccines by the age of 18 months, yet no one knows the long-term risks.

Dr Harris Coulter, who co-wrote *A Shot in the Dark*, said in a later book: 'Developmental (learning) disabilities are nearly always generated by encephalitis. And the primary cause of encephalitis in the United States and other industrialised countries is the childhood vaccination program.'

Some charges against mass immunisation are extraordinary. There's a theory that the AIDS epidemic was triggered by the World Health Organisation's smallpox campaign throughout Africa, Brazil and Haiti—countries that later emerged as having the first wave and highest levels of AIDS. And between 1955 and 1963, 98 million Americans were given a polio vaccine contaminated by a monkey virus that had caused brain cancer in research animals. Why is all this being injected into our babies? The answer lies somewhere between greed and a belief in the greater good.

But mass vaccination is there. It's for the protection of 'the herd'. For it to work, that magic level of 80 per cent of the population must be immunised. That's what makes it a three billion dollar industry worldwide. And there is no shortage of research showing that vaccines are safe and that they are a benefit to society, countering anything that is written against them. We parents are caught in the middle, and the best we can do is make informed decisions on behalf of our children. When Alan was a baby I knew nothing about the dangers and complexities. The National Vaccine Information Center, wanting to help parents make an informed decision and wanting to help them avoid potential dangers, lists eight questions that parents should ask before going ahead with a vaccination:

1   Is my child sick right now?
2   Has my child had a bad reaction to a vaccination before?
3   Does my child have a personal or family history of vaccine reactions, convulsions or neurological disorders, severe allergies, or immune system disorders?
4   Do I know if my child is at high risk of reacting?
5   Do I have full information on the vaccine's side effects?
6   Do I know how to identify a vaccine reaction?
7   Do I know how to report a vaccine reaction?
8   Do I know the vaccine manufacturer's name and lot number?

It is admirable advice that every parent should know.

––––––

I had been in regular contact with Barbara and Kathi over the years, admiring the progress they were achieving, and they called me to let me know about an international conference they were organising. So in September 2000, I went to the International Public Conference on Vaccination, organised by the National Vaccine Information Center, held in Arlington, Virginia. Going there was a chance to see what was happening in the world debate about vaccination. This convention brought together experts from the US, Canada and Europe to talk about new research. It was taking an overall look at the pros and cons of mass immunisation.

I went there not knowing that my life was about to be drastically changed by a new twist of fate. In the months before my trip to the US, I had noticed from time to time that my left arm would feel very heavy. Then I started to notice a feeling like pins and needles in my left leg. I thought I probably had a trapped nerve in my back or was having some problem with my circulation brought on by smoking. A couple of weeks before the trip I mentioned to Kevin that I was having trouble raising my left arm. He said I should go to our doctor and I said I'd leave it until after the US trip. But Kevin insisted I go straight away.

I went to my GP to tell him about it and he did some simple tests and said everything was fine. I left it at that, but a few weeks later I went back again. I was still worried about this numbness, and I was worried about the long flight I would be taking to Washington D.C. in case I had a blood clot. My doctor said he would arrange for me to see a specialist when I came back from my trip, but that I was fine to fly. So off I travelled to America.

I arrived Washington D.C. and made my way to the Sheraton Hotel where Kathi Williams told me, "Vera, you're going to love this. The Department of Health in Ireland have been on the phone to us to know if you are at the convention."

I had never been in Washington D.C. before and I was amazed at the size of the place. The convention was in the Sheraton Hotel. I walked into the conference room and there were banners at tables for all the countries from around the world. There I saw the 'Ireland' table, and throughout the convention I sat at that table on my own. I think it's odd that in Ireland there is no one in the medical profession speaking out against the vaccination programme while in other countries there's so much written and talked about it. The only contribution to the event from the Irish government was the call to find out if I would be attending.

The main topic at the convention was autism. There's a lot of research now into links between vaccination and autism. In the US, 4,500 new cases of autism are diagnosed every year—some states reporting a three to six-fold increase. The condition was first defined in the US in 1943 by a child psychiatrist who had found 11 cases of the new disorder. In Japan the first autistic child was diagnosed the same year that US forces occupied the country and started a compulsory vaccination programme. Problems in the US ranging from attention-deficit hyperactivity disorder to teenage violence are being linked to brain damage caused by the vaccination programme.

Viera Scheibner, an Australian doctor, reported that 'a well-nourished child will go through rubella, whooping cough, chicken pox and the rest with flying colours. Only the vaccinated develop atypical forms of the diseases which are much more dangerous.' There's a whole notion that it's healthier to allow the risk of the diseases, and many people believe that the way vaccinations are given—put directly into the blood stream—not only robs the body of the chance to develop its immunity, but even gets around the body's immune system and makes way for greater dangers. All these vaccinations wear off, and another problem is that adults with no immunity can get the diseases at an age when they are a far greater threat.

Viera had developed a 'Cotwatch' device in doing research on Sudden Infant Death Syndrome—cot death. She found that "the babies' breathing was affected in a certain characteristic manner and over a long period of time (40–65 days) following DPT injections. . . . We also learned from the parents of crib death infants that most commonly the child had died after DPT injection."

Childhood vaccination rates in Australia fell by 50 per cent when the law was changed and they were no longer compulsory. When that happened, cot death rates also fell by half. In 1975, Japan changed the vaccination age to 2 years old. When they did so, cot deaths and infantile convulsions almost disappeared and the country had the lowest rate of infant mortality in the world.

As I sat there through the talks, I was thinking back on all the things that had been said to me down the years in Ireland. Here were scientists and neurologists from all over the world explaining what damage the pertussis vaccine had been causing and how the damage had been caused. All the while as I listened to these people it made me feel more bitter about the way I had been treated in Ireland. I had been rooting everywhere to find research that was being denied in Ireland, and at the convention there were scientists speaking openly about their discoveries on the hidden dangers of mass immunisation.

The openness amazed me. But of course it was the way things ought to be. I had become accustomed, over the years, to having to fight for the truth. I phoned Kevin after the first day of talks and said, "We're living in the dark ages in Ireland."

"That's the way they want to keep us," he said.

One day, in a break from the talks, we were taken for a visit to the House of Congress. One thing I learned is that if an American citizen has a grievance, he can walk in and demand to see his congressman and present his case. American politicians are seen as the servants of the people who elected them. I was fascinated by all that. It was so different from what I had experienced in Ireland.

As far as mass vaccination is concerned, there is an important difference between the way it is treated in the US and in Ireland. In the US vaccination is compulsory and so the State is responsible for the treatment of its citizens. In Ireland vaccination isn't compulsory. If it were, then people could say, 'it was the law and I had to do it so you are to blame for what has happened'. Instead, in Ireland we are told that we have our children vaccinated as a matter of free choice. How can it be a free choice if we don't have all the information? I believe vaccination will never be made compulsory in Ireland—even if the level of people bringing their children for vaccination falls below what's needed to 'protect the herd'. Instead, the medical profession in Ireland will deny the risks and say to people like me, 'prove it in a court of law', while the government will do everything to avoid facing up to the issue.

Over the days of the convention, people got to know me. When I told the people at the convention what I had been through in Ireland, they couldn't believe it. I was asked to give a talk to the convention and I told them my story. I told them about the years of trying to prove the truth of what had happened to Alan, and of how the government and the medical profession had done everything to avoid responsibility. The audience couldn't believe that any country would treat people in my position in that way.

With all these experts around at the event, I was able to ask questions I had long wanted to get answers to and be told the truth. For instance, I had been told that it was impossible that brain damage could be caused by vaccine injections because the chemicals could not cross what is called 'the blood-brain barrier', but an expert told me this was only true if there were no ruptures in the brain and such ruptures could happen with some babies.

I was also told that the drug companies and the State can sometimes set off 'scares' in the community about the urgent need to immunise because of the threat of an epidemic. In the US in 1982, for instance, there had been a television programme warning about the dangers of the whooping cough vaccine. A few months later, whooping cough epidemics were being reported in the states of Maryland and Wisconsin. But an expert, J. Anthony Morris, investigated the 'epidemics' and discovered that in Maryland only 5 of the 41 reported cases were confirmed as whooping cough, and in Wisconsin only 16 of the 43 reported cases were confirmed as whooping cough. All were vaccinated children.

"These scare stories are used to frighten concerned parents into rushing off and getting their children vaccinated," a doctor told me. It becomes a game: when people like me sound the alarm about the dangers, the drug companies or the State find a way to frighten people back into obedience.

There's one thing that has haunted me for a long time now. A doctor I met at the convention sat me down and said, "Vera, I think you are strong enough to hear this." He told me about research that had first come to light in America a few years ago. The children of people of my generation have higher incidence of tumours than children of other generations. There was an investigation of this and CNN revealed these findings. The kind of tumour these children were susceptible to was exactly the kind Renee had. The theory was that a link existed between the vaccinations we were given and this tendency in our babies.

My last day at the convention came and I hadn't had a chance to chat with Congressman Dan Burton. He arranged for his car to pick me up and bring me to his offices on the way to the airport. I was fascinated sitting in this car. It could monitor what cars were around it and what was in the sky above it. Dan told me all about his grandchildren—he is a very loving family man. Dan's biggest concern is the use of mercury in vaccines. Even the Food and Drug Administration knew that, through vaccines, American babies of six months had received more mercury than is considered safe.

"When it sits at your own doorstep it's something else, isn't it?" he said to me. Like the majority of people concerned about vaccination, he is not against the vaccination programme as such, but against the way it is done and the safety standards and screening procedures applied. I was meeting a politician in a position of power who was using his position to discover and publicise the truth. I had met no politician like him in Ireland in my 30 years fighting for Alan.

I came back to Ireland ten times more angry than when I left. I felt like handing in my Irish passport and emigrating. Ireland felt like a dungeon. No matter how hard I tried, I was always faced with a complete denial in Ireland that there could be a link between the vaccine and brain damage. The concern—from the medical profession and from the government—was to find some way of shutting me up. It didn't matter what evidence was put in front of them. The view seemed to be that maybe this could happen in England or Germany or elsewhere in the world, but not in Ireland. And even if they admitted it could happen, they would always say 'but it didn't happen in your case'. Deny, deny, deny.

By this time the UK government was giving an extra £100,000 to the parents of vaccine-damaged children. The principle of giving more financial support to the families had been decided in 1976, but it had taken that long for Rosemary Fox and other dedicated people to finally win the support they deserved. In Ireland, however, the government was still ignoring its responsibility.

———

Within weeks of the trip to the US, I had the appointment with the specialist. He said he would arrange for an MRI scan. An MRI scan is a horrible experience. They put you inside a metal tunnel. I'm very claustrophobic, and the first time I saw the machine I asked them not to put me into it. They coaxed me and assured me it would be all right as long as I remained calm. They said that all they were doing was a scan of my spine. I got a phone call from the specialist saying I needed another scan. This time, to my horror, it was for my head. Alan was brain damaged. Renee died of a brain tumour. And now they wanted to do this scan. Did I have a brain tumour? I asked for sedation going into the machine the second time—your head has to be bolted into place and I was terrified. I was fixed in a collar and my head set in place and I was being pushed into this chamber that's like a metal coffin. You have a panic button, but you are warned that if you use it to stop the process and be taken out, they have to start the whole procedure all over again. The nurse had warned me not to open my eyes, so of course I did inside the chamber and the top of the tube was no more than an inch or two from my nose. Kevin was at the bottom of the tube, and he was patting my foot just to let me know he was there.

The results were ready soon after. We sat down with the specialist and exactly what he said was, "I guess it's multiple sclerosis."

"What's multiple sclerosis?" I asked. This specialist referred me to Donal Costigan, a neurologist. I remember thinking that nothing could be as bad as a brain tumour, so I wasn't too worried. When I saw Donal, he explained what he thought and he used some big medical words I didn't understand.

"Say the words," I said. "Tell me what I have."

"You have multiple sclerosis."

"How do you get rid of it?"

"We'll blow it out of the water with steroids," he said.

"Will that fix it?"

"Well, we'll try it."

It is extremely rare for someone my age to have this condition. Donal kept asking me if I had felt the symptoms years before, but I hadn't. I have always been on the go, and my life has always been full of challenges. I would have noticed the symptoms if I had had them in my thirties. At the time I was first diagnosed, there was a medical conference going on in Dublin about multiple sclerosis, and Donal had presented my case. He came back to me after it and said many of the experts there didn't believe him. They convinced him to do a lumbar puncture on me—the one absolutely certain way of confirming the diagnosis. He did the test and it was positive.

The central nervous system is like the wiring system for your whole body. It is sending signals from the brain all around your body. This 'wiring' has a protective coating. With multiple sclerosis, your own immune system starts attacking the coating and the brain's messages stop reaching their destinations. Your body turns on itself. They don't know why the immune system fails like that, but any connections lost cannot be restored. The illness will never affect my brain or my mind, but it will eventually destroy my central nervous system.

When Alan was destroyed by the pertussis vaccine, I was told that the likelihood of such a thing happening was one in a million. When Renee died of a brain tumour the statistics were probably the same. I was informed in October 2000 that I was one of very few women in Ireland to develop multiple sclerosis of this virulent type at my age. One in a million again? I had buried two children, and now I was diagnosed with an illness that would slowly turn me into a cripple.

I had been recommended to go to a psychiatrist to talk about what was happening to me and so I went. Kevin brought me, and as I left him in the waiting room I said "I'll be either five minutes or an hour with this fella." The psychiatrist was a lovely man, and I talked straight with him.

"Before I even start," I said, "I want you to know that I don't believe in depression and I don't believe in psychiatry. And don't start thinking you can take notes on me, either. I'm here because my doctor wants me to be here and that's all. But if you're man enough to take what I have to say on the chin, then fair dues to you. I hate humanity. It's terrible what's happened to me. I can't cope. How can I be dished out so much?" I told him what the medical profession had done to me and Alan. I told him what the government had done. I told him about Renee. I told him about the multiple sclerosis. "They say now that I'm sick." He said at the end that I didn't need psychiatric help.

———

I spent years learning about vaccines, but I haven't tried to study multiple sclerosis. Only once have I spoken with someone else who has it. Kevin read a magazine article about it, and he quoted me a line from it saying 'the illness does not happen to people over fifty'. Kevin hid the magazine after he read it, but I had watched him. When he went to bed, I sat down and read it. The effects of the illness include double vision, blindness, incontinence, paralysis, loss of speech and loss of balance. All of this was ahead of me.

I had steroid treatment which made me very ill. The only way

I can describe how I felt is to say that I was shut down. I became light-headed and confused, and my vision was distorted. The doctor wasn't absolutely sure that the steroids were causing these problems, but when they gave me a second dose and these reactions became worse, they then decided that the steroid treatment didn't agree with me.

They tried another drug, Imuran, which is a kind of chemotherapy in pill form. I was on it for no more than a couple of days when I started vomiting. Kevin and I had been out for a meal and as we were walking across a bridge on the Liffey I started throwing up. Regardless, I kept taking the pills. At that time we had gone on a trip, and while we were away Kevin had to call in a doctor for me. By the time I got home I was severely ill with diarrhoea and vomiting. To make things worse, I had become completely dehydrated because I hadn't realised that I should have been drinking lots of liquids if I had diarrhoea. I was told to stop taking that medication.

It was then suggested by my neurologist in Dublin that I seek a second opinion in the UK. Kevin and I travelled to London to see him. He examined me and asked me what I thought he could do for me. At that time it had been recommended by the doctors in Dublin that I go on the drug Interferon, a drug which is mainly given to 'relapsing-remitting' MS patients, but mine was 'primary progressive'. He was unsure this would help.

"You know this is chronic progressive and you will lose the use of your arms and your legs," he said. I remember thinking, my God, I've flown to London and paid a £300 fee to sit here in front of this man to hear this. But I didn't show my shock.

Kevin and I walked out to the street and I held on to the railings and my legs buckled under me. I slid to the ground. People had been encouraging me to stay in a positive frame of mind. Then this man had told me bluntly that there was no hope. Kevin kept saying to me, "Forget what he said." We took a taxi to Harrods and went to the café there.

I was given tiny doses of Interferon every couple of days in order to see if I could slowly raise the dose and be able to tolerate it. But when I went on the medication I soon felt I was in a black hole of depression and I couldn't stop crying. I don't know if this drug affects other people this way, but it did me. Kevin contacted the doctor, who said I should stop the treatment immediately.

They then tried chemotherapy. Multiple sclerosis is like cancer in that it is a disease where the body attacks itself. The idea with chemotherapy is to knock out the immune system—the cells that are in fact now attacking your body—in the hope that when those cells grew back they would 'realise' their mistake and the disease would be halted. I was given this every three months, as it takes that long for the immune system to come back. They would knock it on the head again, to re-educate it to stop attacking me. This continued for almost a year and a half until the last time they gave it to me, when I had such a serious reaction that I nearly left this world. But I honestly believe it did stop the disease taking both my arms and my legs. My left side was already affected when this started, but I have been stable since.

The disease is slowly taking my body away from me. I wear a brace that lifts up my left foot. Without it I can't walk because my foot drags on the floor. I need a crutch. I have severe weakness on my left side which makes life very difficult. I hope the disease will never make its way into my right side. There seems to be nothing else out there at present to help me. When I plead with my doctor to help me, he puts his arm around me and gives me a hug.

I once turned on him. "Medical science owes me a life," I said. "You took away my son and you couldn't save my daughter. You can at least do something for me." I phoned up his secretary the next day and asked her to give him a kiss and a hug from me and to say I was sorry. I knew I had hurt his feelings and it wasn't his fault.

I decided to go to Lourdes. I had received no help with my children there, and I wanted to know if it was possible that I could be lucky third time around. Somehow, even since I was a child, I have always believed in miracles. I couldn't resist the idea that there could be a miracle waiting for me in Lourdes.

"Take me to Lourdes when it's closed," I told Kevin. I couldn't bear the thought of going when there might be thousands of people there in case I was recognised again. Kevin talked with a nun who came to his shop to buy bags. The nun explained that Lourdes never closed.

"All right then, take me when there's no pilgrimages there," I said, "and I'll just stand in front of that statue and I'll say 'I'm here, either bloody fix me or don't, because I'm sick of God and I'm sick of religion.'"

Seeing Lourdes again was absolutely horrendous. We hadn't gone with a pilgrimage. We had taken flights that allowed us just to be there for a few days. I couldn't bear again the experience of sitting on an aeroplane reciting rosaries or being part of some group going through all the events and processions. We stayed in a small hotel and kept to ourselves. Just as years before, we would go late at night to the grotto when it was deserted. I wanted to sneak in and out. I didn't want to meet anyone I might know from the times before with Alan or Renee.

When I went to Lourdes, I pleaded. I pleaded for help and for mercy. I had made up my mind that I would only go into the baths once. I went in twice. The first time Kevin had to push me in the wheelchair up to the point where the women helpers took me, undressed me, put me in a sack dress and led me into the water. How I didn't fall apart when they dipped me into the water I do not know. I kept saying to myself "you're tough. You're strong." I walked through the bath to the statue and kissed the feet. Nothing happened. There was no miracle. I looked to Kevin and I thought, is he praying, or is he wishing, or what is going through that poor man's mind? He's looking at me standing here in desperation.

The second time I went into the bath, I started to hate God. I just couldn't understand why God wasn't helping me. When I was leaving Lourdes, I looked at the statue and I spat on the ground. But my mind was in chaos. I was thinking these things, and also thinking, you better say you're sorry. People have been cured in their bedrooms and they've been cured on their way home from Lourdes. But I swore after that that I would never pray again. And I never will.

I was facing a new battle, one happening inside my own body. But as that was beginning, the next legal battle over Alan was coming to an end. My war was still not over, though, and the chance of peace in my life was still beyond reach.

Chapter 9 ∾

| THE VERDICT

In November 2001, the Dublin City Coroner's case reached the Supreme Court. This was his last chance to be freed of the limitations being put on him by the Eastern Health Board—and my chance to continue my fight for justice for Alan. Kevin and I sat through the whole process together.

The court is on the ground floor of the Four Courts building by the River Liffey. It's a very intimidating place. The room itself is enormous and the five judges sat on their grand chairs with Ronan Keane, the Chief Justice, sitting in the centre in the tallest chair. Within ten minutes of the procedures, I had the feeling that the coroner was going to lose his case. I turned to Kevin and told him so, and told him I wanted to leave, but he urged me to stay. The Supreme Court judges are appointed by the State—not by their peers—and I didn't believe they would make a ruling that would work against the State.

I soon felt that the judges did not really understand what they were dealing with. One of the judges commented, "Can these things harm people?" Talking about Alan's pneumonia, another judge leaned over and asked, "Why couldn't they save him. It was only pneumonia." Paul Gardiner showed the last photograph I had taken of Alan, years before his death, when he was already skin and bone. One day we were described as 'vengeful'. The judge reacted to this, pointing out that our son was dead, and the lawyer withdrew the comment.

A considerable time was spent discussing the word 'how', which

I found extraordinary. But you must understand that a coroner's function is to deal with the 'where, when and how'. My point always with Alan was: if it was pneumonia and he was a healthy 22-year old, he would have been saved. But the 'how' just kept going backwards and forwards between both lawyers. It got to the stage where I didn't want to hear the word 'how' any more. There was a reference to another inquest and a court case about it, and the lawyers discussed the difference between 'cause of death' and 'proximate cause of death'. If I hit you with an iron bar and you die, did you die because I hit you with an iron bar or did you die because your brain could no longer maintain life functions due to the fact that your skull was smashed?

Speaking on behalf of his client the coroner, Gerard Hogan SC, said there was no disputing that Alan had died of aspirational pneumonia, but that this was known to be a proximate cause of death and as such was always caused by another condition. The actual cause of the pneumonia was being investigated. If the High Court ruling was upheld, the power of the coroner would be 'highly confined' to the proximate cause of death as against the true cause of death.

Paul Gardiner, speaking on our behalf, followed the same line. If Alan had died a few days after the vaccine, as opposed to 22 years after it, would the coroner still be ordered not to attribute his death to the vaccination? He also referred to the Board's fear of a 'misguided jury', pointing out that the Irish government had placed its trust in juries.

Counsel for the Health Board focused on what the Board believed were the parameters of the coroner's duties. They were of the view that the coroner could only look at the immediate cause of death. They believed that anything beyond that limitation could lead to possibilities of criminal liability or far-reaching public inquiries. In the end, it was up to the five Supreme Court judges to decide whether or not Farrell could continue with the inquest on Alan.

They decided that the coroner had taken too broad an approach to Alan's case. The way the inquest was going, there was a danger of criminal or civil liability being inferred in the verdict and that was against the 1962 Act. The Act also stated that an inquest can establish proximate cause of death but not the broader means of death—a difference referred to was that an inquest could answer the question, how did the death occur, but not the question, how did the person die. They decided the coroner had gone beyond the budget allowed for an inquest by commissioning the expert report. They decided the adjournment, waiting for the report, was too long. They decided that the 1962 Act limited the coroner to summoning no more than one medical practitioner plus a pathologist in an inquest, unless a majority of the jury requested evidence from another medical practitioner. They decided that the coroner's function according to the law was to carry out 'an expeditious and economical inquiry into four limited but significant issues: the identity of the deceased and where, when and how his death occurred'.

Throughout the session, Judge Hardiman kept looking down at me and I felt he was sympathetic to my case. In the end his was the only dissenting voice, saying he agreed on narrow grounds. He said that if a coroner needed more evidence from medical practitioners, "it seems remarkable he cannot obtain it". He also said that he believed the 1962 Act intended to allow juries to comment on possible prejudice to public health, "especially in a time when decisions in many areas are taken by professional and administrative elites whose ability to communicate meaningfully with the general public is sometimes questionable".

The coroner walked away from the Supreme Court with an order instructing him that he could only have one medic and one pathologist give evidence at an inquest. Within days of this ruling, the coroner was presented with a tragic case. A boy had been stabbed and brought for treatment to a GP. The wound was more dangerous than first thought, and the boy's condition worsened.

He was taken to hospital where he died. Six medical witnesses had been called to give evidence, and all would have felt entitled to say their piece in the witness box. The coroner informed the legal representatives that because of the Supreme Court ruling, they had to choose which medic would be allowed to give evidence. All the medics wanted to give evidence from their own point of view. The coroner explained the restriction placed on him. The case had to be put on hold because the lawyers could not select one medic, and so the jury could not hear the case. The mother of the boy fell out of the Coroner's Court in tears. I saw photographs of her and I phoned Brian Hanney, Farrell's assistant, saying, 'Please put your arms around that woman and tell her I'm terribly sorry, but it's not my fault.' If the rule applied to Alan, it had to apply to everyone.

The government decided to set up a review of the duties of a coroner, forming the Coroner's Rules Committee. Kevin and I later made a submission to them. In my opinion the Department of Health would love to come along and say to the coroner, we know we had to stop you on Alan Duffy's case, but carry on as you were before. Another Irish solution to an Irish problem. Brian Farrell would not do that and I still wanted the truth written on Alan's death certificate. Chief Justice Keane, I later read, was once quoted as saying: "Justice delayed is justice denied."

———

After the Supreme Court, I felt that I had not been treated fairly by the legal system. It was then that I started to delve into the European Court of Human Rights in Strasbourg. My own counsel, when I said I couldn't stop trying, told me that in his opinion we had come to the end of the road. But I was determined to find out more. I started researching, and I contacted the offices here of the European Union. They were very helpful, as was the Department of Foreign Affairs.

The European Court of Human Rights exists specifically for people who feel that their rights under the European Convention of Human Rights have been infringed, and who have tried 'all judicial remedies' in their own State. I felt that described our situation.

I put files and information together and finally put the case forward. Weeks later, I received a reply. The case was accepted for consideration. When I found this out, I passed on word to Paul Gardiner. I think he was in shock. "Who did the work for you?" he asked.

"No one," I said. "I did it."

"But it couldn't be."

I had hope again. I had tried and failed over and over again in Ireland. Maybe now, at last, through the European Union I would get justice. Months went by and I sent further material to back up my submission. It then faced a committee of three judges. In September I received a letter saying the application was considered inadmissible by the committee. It was bad enough that they rejected the case, but they also said that they did not enter into correspondence regarding the reasons for their decision. They also couldn't tell me if there was any other avenue. It became another wall. I wrote to the three judges:

> It is now my seventh Christmas and the eighth year I have had to grieve for my dead son Alan not knowing what happened to him.
>
> I turned to you for help. I am entitled to justice and the truth. Money is no use to me or Alan and never was. Maybe that was my mistake. All I ever wanted was the truth.
>
> Alan had no voice and no choice and lost his life as a result. I blindly trusted and now I have to live with that for the rest of my life. I as Alan's mother owe it to him and myself never to stop until I can put him to rest with the truth being told.

I never received a reply to the letter. I think the consequences would be too great if the court agreed with me. 'The common good' wins out, and Alan is just part of the collateral damage.

———

The years rolled on and Alan's case was being bypassed. I'm sure there was a hope that we would just go away. I heard that ferocious pressure was being put on Dr MacMathuna to sign the death certificate, and I heard that Brian Farrell would not accept this. The case was now in his hands and could not be ended by an about-face by the doctor. I wrote to the Medical Council demanding to know how a doctor could be pressurised to change his medical opinion. I never got a reply. I wrote again—in stronger language—wanting to know how and why a doctor would change his opinion after 11 years. Again I received no reply.

In 2005, Kevin and I renewed pressure for the inquest to be completed and finally, in January 2006, the coroner said he would try to reconvene the original jury from 1997. Counsel representing the newly titled Health Service Executive (HSE) called instead for the abandoning of the inquest. He said the Supreme Court ruling had already established that the coroner could not continue to seek a link between Alan's death and the vaccine. The coroner dismissed this, although he acknowledged that he could not consult any more experts. We were in the Coroner's Court the following month, and this time the coroner announced that it was not possible to bring back the original jury and so he would call a new inquest. HSE counsel then made the extraordinary suggestion that the coroner write to Dr MacMathuna and ask him if he would now be willing to sign the death certificate. To my relief, Brian Farrell rejected this completely. It was one small moment of triumph—one time when I felt justice was being done for me and for Alan.

The coroner then set about trying to find a compromise position that would be acceptable to me and to the HSE. His first proposal for Alan's death certificate was:

> Death due to
> (a) Aspirational Pneumonia.
> (b) At the time of contracting Aspirational Pneumonia the deceased was suffering from a Neurological Disorder.
> (c) I am not in a position to determine the cause of the Neurological Disorder.

The HSE rejected this. The coroner then proposed an amendment:

> Death due to
> (a) Aspirational Pneumonia.
> (b) Neurological Disorder (Undetermined).

Kevin and I thought about this and talked with Paul Gardiner about it. We had gone a long, long road and we could see that the HSE were determined not to give way. Poor as this compromise was, we felt it at least left the door somehow open for us and we could move on from the Coroner's Court limbo we had been trapped in for over a decade. So we said we would accept this wording on Alan's death certificate. I was bitterly disappointed, but we would somehow be putting an end to the nightmare.

And what happened next? The HSE objected to the world 'Undetermined'. They weren't going to give an inch on anything. So the coroner suggested his final compromise:

> Death due to
> (a) Aspirational Pneumonia.
> (b) Neurological Disorder.

A date for the final hearing on Alan's case in the Coroner's

Court was set. Kevin and I were determined to fight the proposed verdict.

Up until September 2008, almost 13 years after Alan's death, there was still no death certificate for my son. His name still appeared on the Census form. On 22 September, Kevin and I were back in the Coroner's Court for what we knew would be the announcement of the final verdict on Alan's death. We had a meeting with Paul Gardiner before this, and he told us that our only way out at this stage would be to challenge the coroner's authority to announce a verdict. He had set out with a jury and could not then make a final decision without a jury. It was our last chance to prevent the HSE winning the verdict they wanted—a verdict that would block any link between their vaccination programme and Alan's death.

Counsel for the HSE and Paul Gardiner sat facing each other, with the coroner sitting at his raised bench facing the public. Brian Farrell and Paul Gardiner used the microphones in front of them so that the public could hear them clearly. HSE counsel didn't switch on his microphone and turned to face Farrell when he spoke. As always, there was a representative from Glaxo present who took notes throughout the court hearing.

Brian Farrell obviously thought it was all going to be plain sailing, and he asked for any final comments from either side before pronouncing his verdict. HSE counsel praised him for the verdict he was about to announce, and said that leaving the word 'undetermined' in the verdict would only have been used as fuel by the ill-informed to try making a link between the country's vaccination programme and a health risk to babies. This despite the fact that throughout Alan's medical records there is reference to his neurological damage 'of unknown origin'. Such was the State's fear of any possible questioning of their vaccination programme, that they would deny even the medical professionals in their employ.

Farrell was surprised when Paul Gardiner then informed him

that we would challenge his right to reach a verdict without a jury because he had started the case with a jury. Not sure how to proceed, he halted the session and left the court to consult his legal advisers.

A half-hour later, he was back and announced that he was going to pronounce his verdict as planned. I knew I was powerless to stop him and I just got up and walked out. After he stated his verdict, Brian Farrell apologised 'to Alan's family', saying he knew that the verdict was not what we wanted to hear. Outside, I was in tears while my brother Leonard tried to console me. The HSE had won. They had blocked my attempt, through the Coroner's Court, to win some acknowledgment of the true cause of Alan's death. They had fought every inch of the way—to the Supreme Court and back. I knew they would stop at nothing to block me. By then the HSE had launched an even more aggressive national vaccination programme. The rare case like Alan's didn't matter to them. They would give no apology and tolerate no threat to their master-plan.

After the coroner gave his verdict, Kevin and I sat with Paul Gardiner, who advised us of our options. The coroner had made his decision and a death certificate would be signed. Our only hope was to reject the legality of that verdict. We could start the whole process again, take the coroner to the High Court—challenging his right to give a verdict without a jury when he had started the case with a jury—and presumably wind up again in the Supreme Court. Paul thought it might take four years to get a new inquest, if we were going to be granted one at all.

In my opinion, the HSE had Dr Brian Farrell tied up in knots. In giving his verdict, he read out what is known as his 'draft narrative' of the case. Looking back, I wondered if in that document he had managed to still make some protest because he wrote:

I am of the view that the Inquiry which as stated has been properly and formally and publicly opened and commenced should be brought to a formal and public conclusion in a manner which is consistent both with the Orders of the Superior Courts and with my statutory duty . . .

He did this elsewhere in the document—referring to the fact that the Inquiry had begun 'properly' but omitting that word when referring to the Inquiry being concluded. That certainly was how I felt. But I had exhausted every possibility of getting justice for Alan.

———

In the months after the coroner's verdict, I didn't know what to do. I was trying to cope with my multiple sclerosis and I was trying to get on with my life, but I still could not give up on winning justice for my son. Finally, I decided I was going back to the European Court of Human Rights. The reason was that I had new material. During the time when I was hoping to get a fair hearing in the Coroner's Court, I had received documents from England—documents that had never been presented to the public before—that were Glaxo's own records of reports of vaccine damage they were getting from doctors and hospitals throughout the UK. While Glaxo had always said the vaccines were safe or caused, at most, minor problems, they had their own growing file of damage caused by the triple vaccine. I had been given records from the years 1953 to 1975. There was a total of 131 cases—all of them someone's child. The damage was not, as Glaxo once said, 'sore arms, fever and irritability', but rather convulsions, encephalopathy, coma, rigor, cot death, death, petit mal and grand mal. The reaction time varied from an hour to seven days.

They knew all the time. They had kept their own records. It was a reminder to me of what the medical profession had been openly discussing—at a drug company-sponsored seminar in Dublin—

in the days before I had brought the topic to the front pages of Irish newspapers. They knew, but they didn't want the public to know. They betrayed the public's trust by their lies. Page after page of their records show that betrayal. Rosemary Fox had given me the documents. She had decided not to use them in public in her own battle. But I was ready to go back to the European Court of Human Rights with this evidence.

I then had the great good fortune to meet a very intelligent man, the barrister Gerard Hogan sc. People had recommended to me that I contact Gerard and I had phoned his offices but never got a response. Finally, I started leaving cheekier messages on the phone, saying I'd expect him to at least have the manners to return the phone call. Finally, Gerard called me back. He had stalled meeting with me because of a possible conflict of interest. Once he had been assured that it was all right to help me, he freely gave all the help he could.

I went to meet Gerard in his offices at the Law Library and brought along all kinds of documentation. He smiled, looked over the material and advised me instead to go back with one point only, and to choose the one point that would be least open to getting dragged down in complex debate.

As he put it: "Don't go for the sun, moon and stars, Vera."

"Okay," I said. "We'll go for the stars."

His suggestion was not to go back raising the whole issue of vaccine damage but instead to apply on the basis that Alan had not had a full (a 'proper') inquest because of the limits on the coroner's powers as pointed out by the Supreme Court ruling. It was a wonderful idea, that 'the Farrell decision', reached because the HSE tried to block the coroner from thoroughly seeking to find the cause of Alan's death, could be used to show that Alan's rights were denied and he deserved a new inquest in the light of the changes made to the Coroner's Act.

Gerard advised me that if Alan's case was to be presented to the European Court of Human Rights, it had to be done through legal professionals. I agreed with him. I then needed a solicitor to help me put the submission together and was recommended Michael Finucane. Michael is the son of Pat Finucane, a Belfast solicitor who was murdered in his home in front of his family by loyalists in collusion with the Royal Ulster Constabulary (RUC). Michael, like his father, has dedicated himself to fighting against injustice.

Michael's offices are on Arran Quay and I was very nervous going to meet him. When I arrived at the Quays, I had a phone call from his secretary saying Michael was delayed and I would have to wait. There is a little newsagent and coffee shop near the offices and, as I smoke, the very sweet old man there kindly set up a table and chair from his own kitchen outside the shop for me so that I could have a smoke and a coffee while I waited.

Michael was great at keeping me focused. If I said I 'thought something happened such-and-such a time', he would even shout at me. The facts had to be clear and exact. I became great friends with him because we are two of a kind and he is a rottweiler when it comes to reaching the truth.

Gerard and Michael worked for me and helped me without ever asking for a penny: like me, they weren't in it for the money. All they cared about was the injustice of what had happened. They wanted to help me because their work in the legal profession was driven by their own sense of right and wrong. Gerard has since been raised to the level of judge and is no longer involved in my case. I am eternally grateful to him for all his help. I have been blessed to meet people like him, Michael Finucane and Brian Farrell along the way in my many battles. They care about justice and the truth, which is all I ever wanted for my son. I could not have met two more honourable people than Gerard and Michael.

The process of going to the European Court of Human Rights and getting past first their 'admissibility' stage and to the 'communication' stage could take up to five years. But a win would acknowledge that the coronorial system failed Alan's right to life.

This gave me great hope. But I'm also not finished with the drugs company that destroyed Alan and so many others. I will be going to them with this evidence and I'll see how they respond.

————

Meanwhile, the scandal of the vaccine trials in Ireland has not gone away. In August 2010 the newspapers were full of the story of people who were seeking, through the courts in the US, to get justice for being used in the trials when they were babies in orphanages. The new cover-up led back to a legal block Prof. Irene Hillary made to prevent the full story being told.

In 2000, the chief medical officer Dr James Kiely delivered the report, ordered by then Minister for Health Brian Cowen, about the vaccine trials in 1960/61, 1970 and 1973. This report revealed that there were gaps in knowledge: most particularly, had the children's parents and guardians been fully informed of the trials and given permission? There were also discrepancies in dates and permissions for the 1973 trials. As the report said:

> Examination of the documentation provided by Wellcome shows that, while what appears to be the Eastern Health Board's initial correspondence with Dr Griffith in Wellcome is dated August 1973, the trial itself was apparently in progress earlier in 1973. It appears that a number of blood samples for use in the trial were taken as early as February 1973. Further, a letter of no objection to the trial and to the utilisation of the modified vaccines had been given to Wellcome in April 1973 by Dr A. Scott of the National Drugs Advisory Board on foot of the submission of a protocol specifically for this trial from Wellcome Laboratories prior to this.

By this time, as a result of the shocking revelations about physical and sexual abuse of children in the State's care, a 'Commission to inquire into Child Abuse' had been formed. The country had no stomach for yet another betrayal of Irish children, and Cowen's successor Micheál Martin referred the vaccine trials report to the Commission. A separate section of the Commission would devote itself to investigating the vaccine trials.

So far, so good. It looked like the Irish government was finally taking on full and open responsibility for how it treated the nation's children. Information was being gathered and by 2003 the Commission was ready to start holding public hearings.

Prof. Irene Hillary had carried out all three trials; Prof. Meenan had worked on two of them. They both challenged the High Court orders instructing them to give evidence to the Commission and their objections were upheld. And then came the Irish twist. The government did not object to this prevention of work in a Commission it had itself set up. New Minister for Health Mary Harney instead ordered that the vaccine 'module' of the Commission be closed down. This even despite the fact that the Commission had received a huge amount of information from the drugs company to help with the investigation— information that would never be presented to the public because the Commission had been closed down. Business as usual in Ireland: hide the truth.

Mari Steed, an Irish woman now living in the US, was one of the orphan babies used in the vaccine trial in Cork in 1960 and 1961. She and three other victims of the trials started a legal action against Glaxo Smith Kline (Wellcome when the trials were being done). I hope they succeed in getting justice. But I also wish that a day would come when Irish people can get justice in Ireland and not have to go through endless battles—or to other countries—to have what is rightfully theirs.

Then Patricia McDonagh, writing for the *Irish Independent*, brought even more scandal to light. Philip Delaney, who had been adopted in 1965 in Cork, had discovered that he was used in a 'five-in-one' vaccine trial. The extraordinary thing was that, although he had documentation to prove this had happened to him, no medical researcher or drugs company would come forward saying the work was done by or for them. These were secret, unauthorised, anonymous drug trials on Irish babies being used as fodder.

———

And while these people looked back decades to seek the truth and to get justice, yet another vaccine scandal broke out when Sarah-Kate Templeton, health editor of the *Sunday Times*, revealed a whole new wave of vaccine damage recorded in the UK from 2003 onwards. Through the Freedom of Information Act she received records showing that:

> Forty children are suspected to have died as a result of receiving routine vaccines in the past seven years. Childhood vaccines are also suspected of having left two young children with brain injuries and caused more than 1,500 other neurological reactions, including 11 cases of inflammation of the brain, 13 cases of epilepsy and a coma.

In a response that goes all the way back to Brendan O'Donnell and the Eastern Health Board in Ireland in 1973, the UK's Medicines and Healthcare products Regulatory Authority (MHRA) said that this should be seen 'in the context of the 90 million doses of childhood vaccines given in that time'. One in a million? More? Less?

The MHRA were responding to a list of questions that they answered openly, clearly and in great detail. These questions were:

1. Can you please tell me how many reports you have received

of adverse reactions to the MMR vaccine since January 2003?

2. Can you please tell me how many reports you have received of brain damage as an adverse reaction to the MMR vaccine since January 2003?

3. Can you please tell me how many reports you have received of death resulting from MMR vaccine since January 2003?

4. Can you please tell me how many reports you have received of adverse reactions to childhood vaccines excluding MMR since January 2003?

5. Can you please tell me how many reports you have received of brain damage as an adverse reaction to childhood vaccines since January 2003?

6. Can you please tell me how many reports you have received of serious injury as an adverse reaction to childhood vaccines since January 2003?

7. Can you please tell me how many reports you have received of death resulting as an adverse reaction to childhood vaccines since January 2003?

Seeing how all this had been brought out in the open in the UK by a simple approach to a government body, I wrote to the Irish Medical Board with the exact same set of questions. I expected a written response with details provided in the same manner as the MHRA, who gave lists and charts. Instead, I got a phone call from the IMB asking me why I wanted this information and telling me that they would like to discuss the matter with me.

In due course they gave their answer. Unlike the UK, the Irish

Medical Board gave lump figures instead of detailed accounts of adverse reactions to vaccines. Even so, there were deaths and severe reactions recorded. I have since been asking them to follow up with the kind of statistics provided in the UK to the same questions. The IMB wrote back telling me they will do so, though I have not yet had that detailed reply. At least now there is an open exchange.

By early 2011 any progress I had hoped for was still out of reach. I had hoped for a positive ending to this book, but it is not to be. Early in the year, Michael Finucane phoned me and asked if he could come to my home to chat with me. He wouldn't tell me what it was about. When he sat down with me, he was distraught. He broke the news to me: the European Court of Human Rights had turned down my appeal.

Alan's case had been presented to the ECHR by the best legal brains in the country. Indeed, Gerard Hogan has since been appointed a judge of the High Court. We knew that what we were presenting was a case dealing with the suppression of the truth. Two examples were submitted. Now, think what that organisation in Brussels calls itself: the 'European Court of Human Rights'. From my point of view, my rights were trampled on and the right to life of my son was trampled on. After a year, with no reason given—they never give a reason—and no indication of whether we can go back with the case again. The news devastated me totally as now I know I will never get an honest inquest in Ireland.

I knew that the ECHR were in a situation with Alan's case of being 'damned if they do, damned if they don't'. They took the easy way out. Alan and I were less of a threat than the Irish State. I had sent the ECHR all the research I have written in this book regarding vaccination trials and pharmaceutical information. I read the pamphlet that gives the rules of the Court, and in it is stated that all governments have an obligation to their citizens to keep them safe from infectious diseases. So, sorry Vera and Alan, you do not fit in with our rules.

So do I consider Alan and the rest of the children damaged by vaccines to be collateral damage? Sacrificial lambs to protect the herd? It is a matter of the common good again. It is a scary thought.

I wasn't alone in my frustrations. In May 2011 Dr Brian Farrell, speaking at a conference on inquests which was held in Dublin, called on the Minister for Justice of the new Irish government to reintroduce the Coroner's Bill 2007. The legislation had been drawn up in response to the coroner's case going to the Supreme Court, but it had never been voted into effect. The new coalition government of Fine Gael and Labour did not keep it on their legislative programme.

Fiona Gartland, reporting for *The Irish Times*, quoted Dr Farrell as saying:

The Coroner's Bill 2007 was needed as soon as possible to ensure Ireland complied with European jurisprudence and with its obligations under Article 2 of the European Convention on Human Rights.

It was designed to provide a legal framework for conducting inquests in compliance with the convention. It would also provide coroners in the State with increased investigative powers and address shortfalls in the domestic law regarding inquests.

Under the European convention the State has an obligation to hold a public inquiry where a death occurs of an individual or individuals in the care or custody of the State or when the death is caused by agents of the State.

In that last comment, Dr Farrell summed up exactly the manner in which the Irish State had failed Alan.

| LOOKING FOR MEANING

I have a children's shop in Dublin city and sometimes in years gone by—I don't do it any more—I would see young mothers with their babies and ask them if they were going to have their child immunised. The young mothers are usually proud to say they will have their babies immunised. They are uninformed and naive. They don't know the dangers. And they are the ones who keep the critical level of immunisation up in us—'the herd'—and keep certain diseases under control. Their ignorance is what keeps the system running at the required level of vaccination. After Alan's experience, none of my children or grandchildren has had any vaccinations.

Back at the time I brought Alan for his vaccinations, I was living in ignorance. That ignorance was encouraged by the medics and the State. Sometimes I blame myself for not knowing more back then. I sat my son on my lap as they injected that poison into him. I wheeled him there and wheeled him back. But I was a working-class mother and no one informed me or listened to me. I believe to this day that Alan was either used in the trials of new vaccines or was given the animal vaccine. What is absolutely certain is that, with my family history of epilepsy, he should not have been given the pertussis vaccine in the first place. Was I warned of that risk? No. Where is the honesty and caring and compassion I thought should come naturally to people in the medical profession? I've seen little of it down the years. I have no respect left for the medical profession. How could I when I've witnessed their twists and turns down the years?

In 1998 the Association of General Practitioners were saying they were afraid of continuing the national vaccination programme unless parents were given a full list of the possible side effects of vaccines. In 1975 that was one of the first things I asked for when we set up the Association for Vaccine-Damaged Children. In 1998 the doctors said parents must sign a consent form so that the doctors could not be sued in the event of damage. In 1975 I wanted the form so that parents would know just what risks were being taken with their children's health and safety.

If there has to be a risk involved in vaccination, then so be it. But people should be informed as to exactly what risks they are taking so they may make informed decisions for themselves. That has never been the policy in Ireland. If the government can keep people uninformed and thereby keep the immunisation level up to 80 per cent then they are home and dry.

Nobody has the right to say: "There's a hundred children. We're going to vaccinate them all, but we know that one of them will be brain damaged. We don't know which one, but we're going to do it anyway." The medical profession seem to feel they have such a right, and that we should not question them. The other alternative is to not vaccinate at all, and I don't know what would happen then. But until they find a safe vaccine, the least they can do is admit to the risks and keep parents fully informed.

One life is too many. Only almighty God has the right to take or give life. Doctors, drug companies and politicians play God and then try to ignore what happens to someone like my son Alan. I won't let them. And I will never forgive them. They destroyed my life by turning my search for the truth into an endless battle. I need to know what killed my son. I know that a perfectly healthy baby doesn't suddenly turn into a screeching, withdrawn infant with massive brain damage. But no one is helping me find the truth. If Alan had been murdered there would be a police investigation. But even Alan's inquest was thwarted on the grounds that Irish justice said the inquest was trying to look too deeply into what had happened to him.

All I ever wanted was an apology from the Irish government and the medical profession for what they did to my son. But over the years I've realised that they couldn't say sorry. It's not that they wouldn't. They simply couldn't. They must protect their vaccination programme. My friend Kathi Williams in the US calls it 'their sacred cow'. There's a huge lie at the heart of the idea of vaccinating populations, and people like me, Rosemary Fox and Kathi Williams have forced the truth to the surface. But in Ireland that truth is still being denied.

We get what we deserve in this country. To me, authorities and governments are servants to the public. The same applies to the medical profession. That means that in Ireland I stick out like a sore thumb. I don't conform to what I've been told. I have to have answers. I have to have things explained. I was like that before what happened to Alan, but I have become more extreme over the years. It makes me a nuisance, because I refuse to go away and do what I'm told.

The medical profession and the pharmaceutical companies would have been learning time and again of stories like Alan's, but they did not come forward to sound an alarm. They had to be forced into admitting the truth. I'll never understand that. I've long ago learned that medicine is not something to be trusted blindly. Why must the risks always be hidden or denied?

I have seen the medical experts run rings round the public. The pharmaceutical business is huge and has huge influence. Before all the controversy—when the mothers of the herd were showing up without questions to have their children jabbed—the medical profession here was more open about the dangers. Now, because it suits them, the experts say that the fears of damage through vaccine that were being talked about back in the 70s were a false alarm. They say the acellular form of the pertussis vaccine is safer. Very good. And I have seen all kinds of research saying how much safer it is. But *safer than what?* The very fact that they researched for decades to find this new pertussis vaccine is evidence that they knew there was a problem.

Rosemary Fox carries on with her work and maintains an active pressure group. Thanks to her, the families of vaccine-damaged children have received higher amounts of State financial support over the years. There is now so much contradictory research, however, that there is no longer solid ground on which to build a claim against the pharmaceutical companies. Meanwhile, doctors in the UK get a £1,800 annual bonus if they achieve a 90 per cent vaccination rate, and there have been reports of doctors striking families off their list because the family would not agree to have a child vaccinated. The only real difference between the UK and Ireland is that the government there has been more willing to be supportive of the victims, although the campaign to establish a link between the MMR vaccine and autism has lost State financial aid.

I have often wondered if I hadn't been so public would I have got further. I don't know. Why is it that people who speak out in Ireland are considered trouble-makers? Sometimes I think the Irish always take things personally and go on the defence instead of admitting there's a problem—whether or not they are part of the problem. The years and my experiences have made me harder and quicker to speak out. To me, that means I have no reluctance about demanding what I believe is my right. We should all be doing the same. That wouldn't make trouble; that would make things better.

I've seen with doctors that if they think they've made a mistake, then their first reaction is to deny there could possibly have been a mistake. They end up defending lies and maybe telling more lies to cover up for the first lie, and on and on. The truth gets buried along with our children. Almost all the medics I've met have fought long and hard to defend their profession and were quick to write me off as a crank. It seems—as shown with other scandals—that the truth in this country is the last resort and is only ever revealed grudgingly or unwillingly. One day it will all come out, because lies never go away.

Will I ever be able to establish what they did to Alan? It's probably too late, now that he is dead. The only way my case could be proven now would be if the government and the drug companies decided to come clean and release all their files and the facts they have been hiding. I believe that when I realised what had happened to Alan and raised the alarm, some government official had a conversation or correspondence with some drug company official in which the mistake was acknowledged. But no one has ever stepped forward. The truth is not offered by these people.

I believe the Eastern Health Board know what they did to Alan, but they can never admit it. I am convinced Alan was either used in a medical trial or that the batch he was given was too toxic. I believe this because I have seen, over the years, how the vaccine damaged other children. It was never total destruction—there were degrees of damage. I came across another boy who had been given the same vaccination batch as Alan and he was brain-damaged, but I never saw anyone as completely destroyed as Alan.

I have no doubt about it: Alan was destroyed by the pertussis vaccine. I call it science gone mad, but remember it was not until 1987 that Ireland brought in legislation to monitor drugs trials. Up until then we had vaccine trials on the most vulnerable. I know that Alan was not the only child destroyed by vaccine, and my mission has been to make people aware and to have the State admit the dangers. I know that Alan's story has helped people to be more aware of the dangers of vaccines.

Thirty-five years of my life and Kevin's life went into our battle for Alan. Will I succeed? Yes, I will. How long will it take? I do not know. Time is irrelevant. Irish people are a wonderful race, but unfortunately they don't stand up for their rights and they let these people walk all over them. We allow these people to cover up when they know the truth. If I could get this information about the pharmaceutical companies, then I am fully sure the State had it too. Britain paid £9 million to victims in 1998. Germany, the US, Japan—most civilised countries—recognised that these vaccines were very dirty and toxic. In the decades up to the 80s, thousands of babies worldwide were damaged. But somehow, magically, not in Ireland. Our babies are unique. Our government says our babies don't suffer vaccine damage. I have grown to hate this country I was born in. It cost me my son Alan's life and probably my health.

If the World Health Organization wants mass vaccines, then it has an obligation to force the pharmaceutical companies to make safer ones. Vaccines have done a lot of good, but also terrible damage. The system established in the US—of putting a tax on every shot to create a fund to support vaccine-damaged children—should be applied everywhere. The system is not litigious, so no lawyers are getting rich on human tragedy, and the drug companies can do their work while acknowledging the risks instead of trying always to hide the truth for fear of the consequences. No adverse publicity; no cover-up. But it's a bitter pill for the drug companies to swallow.

I have recently started talking to EU representatives in Brussels about adopting the US system here. If the wish is to keep the world free of infectious diseases, and if mass vaccination can bring some benefits but also brings risks, then the price must be paid. No mother should have to go through what the Irish government put me through. I only ever wanted an apology and the truth, not the taxpayers' money. It was not the taxpayers' fault.

I consider vaccines a necessary evil. All mothers need to educate themselves and get full information before agreeing to a vaccine for their child. Your GP is trained to convince you how good vaccines are and will do everything to convince you. A question I would ask of any GP would be: write me a letter stating these things are completely safe and that you will take responsibility if my child is destroyed. I bet no such letter would be written.

What happened to me can happen to you and your child. Vaccines carry a risk of death or severe brain damage and this was always known in medical circles. But it's like a war on disease: there will be some innocent victims and when that happens a trail of lies will follow from the very highest to the ordinary general practitioner. It is an unspoken understanding in the medical profession and the government. After all, they can only think of *the common good.*

———

I have been trying for decades to get justice for Alan. In that time I've seen how other countries have addressed the problem and given financial support to the parents of vaccine-damaged children. Rosemary Fox was, very deservedly, awarded an MBE. The Irish government, meanwhile, would not grant me as much as the word 'undetermined' on my son's death certificate as some kind of acknowledgment in their eyes of a possible link between his death and their vaccine programme.

Meanwhile, the acellular version of the pertussis vaccine is now the one used in Ireland. But there have been two other changes: the HSE say there are no contra-indications; and vaccination starts at two months instead of five. The HSE guidelines state:

> Note: *The following are no longer regarded either as contra-indications or precautions. They have not been shown to cause permanent harm and are significantly less common after acellular than after whole-cell vaccines;*

1. Temperature of more than 40.5° within 48 hours of dose of a pertussis-containing vaccine.
2. Hypotonic-hyporesponsive episode within 48 hours of a previous dose of a pertussis-containing vaccine.

3   Seizures within 72 hours of a previous dose of a pertussis-
    containing vaccine.
4. Persistent, inconsolable crying lasting more than three
    hours within 48 hours of a previous dose of a pertussis-
    containing vaccine.

All of the above describe effects on Alan and other babies
damaged by the whole-cell pertussis vaccine. The only accepted
contra-indication is anaphylaxis, which is an instant, extreme and
potentially fatal allergic reaction that would happen under the
doctor's nose after giving the injection. And I wonder why the
vaccinations now start when the baby is two months old? Could
it be that at such an early age a reversal in the baby's development
would be far more difficult to detect? If any damage were caused,
it would all be done before the baby reached six months. Is this
medical progress?

There are three sets of solid facts that I can present here. They
are written evidence of behaviour by the medical profession that
could at the very least be called 'wrong'.

One:
To begin with, the documented facts of Alan's third vaccine
injection:

(1) I was expressing concerns about Alan to doctors and to the
    district nurse from after his first injection.
(2) On 10 January 1974 the district nurse—who up to then had
    been very happy with Alan's development—noted in her
    report 'infant not sitting alone, falling to one side, not
    grasping objects or taking anything in his hand'.
(3) The paediatrician Neil O'Doherty, seeing Alan in January
    at the Edenmore Health Clinic, noted that he had
    'developmental delay of obscure origin and hypotosis'.
(4) A January internal memo from the Eastern Health Board to

'each immunisation doctor and all members of the immunisation staff' stated: 'If you learn that after a previous injection the child was unnaturally limp or drowsy, or had a convulsion or any other sign of encephalopathy, a further injection must not be given . . .'

(5) On 6 February, despite my protests and concerns and despite all the documented facts and warnings stated above, Alan was given his third injection, the one that I believe really destroyed him.

Alan should not have been vaccinated for whooping cough—and certainly should not have received the third injection.

Two:
The other documented event concerns the way in which evidence that would help prove what happened to Alan is being hidden.

In 1989, according to the Department of Health, all records pertaining to Alan from the Edenmore Health Clinic were destroyed in a fire. As I wrote to the Minister for Health at the time: 'Is the Department of Health asking me to believe that with all the fuss we were creating since 1974, including meetings with your predecessors Mr Corish, Mr Haughey and Mr O'Connell, that our files were lost/destroyed by fire?' As far back as the mid-70s, Corish was quoted as saying he had requested copies of all files relating to Alan. In my letter I asked for exact details of when the fire happened and what the fire brigade or police report said about it. I asked for the name of the person within the Department who had searched for copies of Alan's files elsewhere but had failed to find any. There was never a reply to my letter.

Three:

The third point is a matter of what has been left unsaid by Glaxo Wellcome. It is now known that in the late 60s and up to the mid-70s in Ireland there were experiments being carried out here on children. There were also animal vaccines being used on children and—as in the Best case— there were toxic vaccines being used on children. Why can't Wellcome be open and honest with people like me and give us their records on the vaccines our children were given? Why can't they be open with this grieving mother and assure me that they took every precaution that the vaccine they supplied was safe and that I am wrong to suspect their vaccine? Did batches 85274, 85401 and 85404—the batches used on Alan—pass all their laboratory tests for safety? Around the time Alan was being vaccinated, the Eastern Health Board were writing to Wellcome saying there was a huge increase in side effects from the vaccines. Was Alan one such case that was reported?

For decades I have fought against the brick wall of political and medical interests telling me to 'prove it'. But why can't I put the same question to them? If governments and the medical profession and the pharmaceutical companies consider themselves to be entrusted with the health and welfare of the people, then why can't *they* prove to *me*—a woman who believes she lost her son because of them—that I am wrong. Why, instead of dodging and denying and concealing, can't they come to me and say, "Here is the proof that we did everything correctly and we had nothing to do with the misfortunes and death of your son." Why can't they put my mind to rest? Why can't they be completely open-handed and prove that they deserve to be entrusted with the welfare of our children? Why can't they say, "We were given the responsibility to take care of the health and welfare of these babies, so here's the proof that we did that." If they truly cared, then wouldn't they want to know if they had made a mistake? Wouldn't they want to learn from the mistake and acknowledge it so that they could deserve our continued trust? What are they afraid of? I am not afraid to accuse them of my son's destruction and death. Are they afraid to step forward, with full disclosure of all the facts, to prove I am wrong? It would prove their credibility and trustworthiness.

They haven't done it so far. They have just found ways to treat me and people like me as some kind of pests. I have always thought that one reason they have fought so hard to refute my claims is that they don't understand my motives. I don't want their money. All I want is the truth. Money could not have changed Alan's life. What would I have done with money if I had been given some award for him? I couldn't make his life better. Could I buy myself a villa somewhere and sit there and think to myself, Alan's condition gave me this. I couldn't bear that. I always thought that if I ever got the case into court and then received an award, I would give the money to cancer research in memory of Renee.

Deep down, I know I blame myself for what happened to Alan. I think about the unbelievable suffering he had and I feel that if I had known more I could have saved him from all that. But the vaccine was a hidden enemy. It wasn't as if there was a baby food on the market that had been banned in some other country and I had used it regardless. This was medicine and I had trusted the medical profession to use it properly and safely. The problem is that they didn't merit my trust. I am still angry that I trusted people who didn't respect the trust given to them. I am still angry that I lined up with the other mothers, all of us believing that these doctors and nurses knew more about our children's welfare, when in fact to them we were just 'the herd'. I think I have turned a lot of that anger in on myself. I sometimes blame myself for what happened to Renee—was it because I was angry and fighting over Alan when I was carrying her that she got the tumour? There have been times when I have felt angry with my mother. When my sister Anna was vaccinated she had a massive epileptic fit and my mother was told that she should have no more vaccinations. My mother was annoyed. She thought Anna was being deprived of something. My mother never told me that. She had asked the doctors at the time if the injection had caused the epilepsy, and they said it hadn't, so she thought nothing more about it.

Modern medicine destroyed my son, couldn't save my daughter, and has not been able to help me. No matter what they try, nothing works to heal or halt my multiple sclerosis. It's like there's a wall around me and nobody will cure this other than the Almighty. I don't know what is ahead for me. I feel God holds me in his hand. I curse him and I damn him and I feel he is up there laughing.

There was a time when, before I'd go to sleep at night, I'd say to myself, nothing else can happen to me now. Two of my children are gone, but my children Tracey, Olga, Karl and Kevin are safe. Kevin and I are safe. Nothing worse can happen than what I have been through, and there are two angels taking care of us now. Yet multiple sclerosis is the most terrible thing that could have been thrown at me. I always loved my style and good shoes and fashion. I loved dancing. It hasn't destroyed my confidence because it has made me more aware of myself. I will bow to nobody and I am impressed by nothing.

Some people can watch a film or read a story and it makes them cry. Nothing makes me cry. I feel now that I'm on the outside looking in. I find I can't even talk with friends any more, because no one else has enough in common with me. They can talk about their holidays or the new clothes they've bought. But that trivial girlie thing is gone. My life is somewhere else. I can't listen to people complaining about the small things of life. They should realise how lucky they are to be healthy and alive and to have healthy and happy loved ones.

Sometimes I wonder if I should commit suicide. But even

though I think about it, I know I couldn't do that. My work is not finished yet. I can imagine people saying, why would she do that? I thought she was stronger than that. Imagine she gave in after all.

I place no value on owning things. I would live happily in a little hut if I could have my children back. But I can't have that. Still, I feel that Alan is with me. In all the years since Alan's death, there have been times when I would suddenly get a beautiful smell and I would think, he's here, and I would say hello to him. There was once, I believe, a time when our son Alan came back us. A couple of years after Alan's death, Kevin and I went on a family holiday to Florida with our three youngest, Olga, Karl and Kevin. One night we went out for a family meal in a Chinese restaurant. We booked a cab to bring us back to the hotel. It was night-time, and we were on a motorway when the driver drove straight through a red light across five lanes of speeding cars. Cars were swerving everywhere. I dived on top of the children to try and protect them. Kevin had grabbed the dashboard and was trying to brace himself for impact. I thought we were all going to die. The cab hit the kerb and I thought it was going to turn over. We reached the other side, car horns blaring and cars screeching past us.

The cab driver apologised. He said he had blanked out for a second and run the red light. Kevin said there was no point starting an argument with the driver. We were taken to the hotel, and it was only then that Kevin read the driver the riot act. "You nearly killed my whole family," Kevin roared at him.

We went to our room. I had a cigarette, as usual, then went asleep. Kevin stayed up. The next day he was in a very odd mood.

"What's going on with you?" I finally said.

"I don't know if I should talk to you about it," he said.

I coaxed him, and he told me what was troubling him.

"After the fright of the near crash, I couldn't sleep," he said. "I was sitting up, looking at you asleep, thinking that Tracey back in Ireland could have been the only member of the family left alive.

And then Alan spoke to me."

Kevin started crying.

"Alan spoke to you?" I said. "Kevin, you were asleep."

"How could I be asleep sitting up smoking a cigarette and looking at you."

"What makes you think it was Alan?"

"He said his name."

"What did Alan say?"

"He said, 'Dad, how could you think for a minute that you were in danger. I'm with you all everywhere you go.' And he said, 'Tell Mam she's right in what she's doing and what she says happened to me is the truth.'"

"What did he sound like?" I asked Kevin.

"He sounded a bit like Karl, but not the same. He sounded like a young man," Kevin said. "He told me to tell you that he loves you very much and that he's very happy where he is."

Kevin is always steady and clear and would never speak anything other than facts. When I saw how moved he was, I believed him. Alan really had spoken to him.

———

I will never leave this country, although I would love to. I would feel I am leaving my two children behind. After all, they are buried in Irish soil. Someone said to me once, "You have two angels looking after you now. Nothing more can happen." How ridiculous that was. If I was asked if I believe in God, I would have to say no. I believe in nothing—only in what I can see. Something would have to drop from heaven—if there is such a place—and speak to me before I would change my mind. I say to Kevin, "If I die first, put me in a field. I will never cross the doors of a church as long as I live, so don't take me there when I am dead."

I have never gone back to Renee and Alan's grave. Sometimes I drive to a vantage point up on Howth Head where I can look down on the cemetery. I know exactly where their grave is. I sit there and think about them. Sometimes too I think of just putting my foot on the accelerator and driving off the cliff. Then I'd think, then maybe I'd burn to death, and I'd hate to burn to death. But always in the end I think, no. I have more to do. It's not over.

I cannot forget all the yesterdays and I cannot face all the tomorrows. I live now in a twilight zone. I can't let go of what has happened—to Alan, to Renee, to us as a family—and I can't bear to think of what lies ahead with this illness. I am angry and I don't want to let go of that anger. I feel it keeps me going, and yet I wonder if I let go of the anger would my immune system realise its mistake and my multiple sclerosis might stop.

Kevin tells me I have saved thousands of children by raising the alarm about the dangers of vaccination. It's no consolation for me. I lost my son. He was our flesh and blood. Kevin says that maybe something like this had to happen to someone like me for things to change. Maybe so. But God has offered me no consolation. Instead, I have been given this illness with no way of beating it. I try to trust God. I try to be able to say, 'Take my arms, take my legs, do what you want. It's your will.' To do that, I have to let go of my anger. If I do that, I think I'll die. I won't let go. I never have and I never will.

So where now? I am dealing with politicians in Ireland and in Brussels trying to make this a European issue. My ultimate goal is to get the same system in all of Europe that exists in America: a tax on every vaccine to create a fund for compensating vaccine-damaged children. Vaccination is important and necessary. I would never deny that. They cause damage, but they also save lives. I have gone past any wish for revenge and now see the hope that I might be able to do some good. If I succeed in getting this change made, it will be the high point of my life.

I hope this book has interested and educated you. I hope you have healthy, happy children and never have to go through what

Kevin and I went through because of the Irish government. If both my aims fail—seeking justice from the Irish legal system and from the drugs companies—I would have to conclude that Ireland must be the most dangerous place in the world to have a child. The vaccination programme has been protected through lies and deceit. Somebody had to say stop, and that was me.

There's one last thing I want to add. For all that has happened to me, the only good thing I can say about my life is that I married Kevin. He is an amazing individual and a wonderful man. He has always been romantic and thoughtful, and down the years he has always idolised our children and me. I have been so close to the edge so many times, and he has always dragged me back. He knows my every mood. He knows me better than I know myself. I know that if he died I would go with him instantly. I wouldn't want to breathe without him. I have never seen in any other couple the intensity of what Kevin and I have. People have often told me that they loved to see me and Kevin dance—that there was something specially magic about it. Of course now, with my illness, I can't dance any more. Indeed, Kevin had wanted us to renew our marriage vows and have another big wedding, but when the multiple sclerosis struck me, I said I wouldn't do it. I wouldn't go dragging my leg down an aisle with people watching me. It would tear me asunder to walk up the aisle to him in this state, thinking of all that's happened over the years. Our daughter Tracey tried to convince me to do it, but I wouldn't change my mind.

Kevin is always watching out for me and he has been my support. I don't know how he has lived through all this. Neither of us deserves what has happened, but he has remained a kind man. I admire the kindness in him and the love he has for his family. Kevin adores children, and I can hardly imagine how painful it must have been for him to see what happened to Alan and Renee. He kept it all in. He supported me when I cried. He couldn't fall asunder in even the hardest of times because he was my strength.

What troubles me, though, is that I can never understand why Kevin has had to endure so much. For such a wonderful family man to lose two children. For such a great husband to see multiple sclerosis taking his wife. As my condition gets worse, Kevin is the only person who can make me laugh. Always, he's the one who is there for me. He has done nothing to deserve such tragedy. Neither have I. Maybe the last words are the ones chosen for the headstone of our children's grave: God works in mysterious ways.

AFTERWORD

PRODUCT RECALL

Vaccines have harmed thousands, yet the best we can hope for is that the State informs the pharmaceutical companies. But nothing changes. Imagine a product in a supermarket causing upset stomachs or something trivial. It would immediately be recalled by the manufacturer. Not so with vaccines. I consider it to be like a war: innocents die. Vaccines fight a war on disease. It never fails to shock me when the powers that be say, 'well, we vaccinated 90 million successfully' as if a percentage of lives destroyed did not matter. Until it is your child. Doctors are all aware of the dangers, but they are told to push vaccines as much as possible. Their answer will always be: 'The advantages outweigh the risks.'

People often ask me if I am against vaccines. I am not. It is all we have for now until something better comes along. God help any doctor who speaks out about their dangers. They will be crucified or worse—struck off. I am a private citizen who could not be bought or shut up, and I live in a democracy. Ireland is the only country I know of which is the best at covering up shocking scandals. Would you let your child climb a tree, go out on a branch with the risk that that branch might break, with no safety net to catch them? I do not think so. Over the years I have come across a lot of information which I have written about. It shows that the State knew, and the readers of this tragic story are entitled to see what I found.

Now I would like to go more into the trials that were carried out in this country by Glaxo Wellcome. What arrogance this State had to give the go-ahead to do such a thing: breaking the Geneva Convention and abusing children. What better place than mother and baby homes. Whether permission was given or not, these mothers were in a very vulnerable position, being cared for by the State until someone adopted their child—if that was what they wanted. As if that was not bad enough, the State got even 'braver' and used 60 children from private families in the Dublin area. It would be my educated guess that they did not go to affluent areas. That would be too risky: the working-class built-up sprawling areas would do nicely. 'How did this happen to our children?' was the newspaper headline when it was discovered that a cow vaccine had been administered to 90 children by mistake. But who were the children, and who is to know what that will do to them in later life? Maybe nothing, or maybe something very serious. Nobody can know. It will, of course, be said that it was a sign of the times we lived in, but that's no excuse. How many scandals are put down to 'a sign of the times we lived in'? Alan could have fit into any of these situations and God knows how many others.

I am a very private individual whose sense of justice forced my hand to let other mothers know what no doctor or the State will tell you. Alan is dead 17 years now and I still have no closure. A death certificate was issued. It will never take residence under my roof because it is not the truth. What will Strasbourg rule on the State or on Alan? I believe they will be damned if they do and damned if they don't. I am only one who could not be broken. We need safer vaccines and the laws changed to protect the ones who suffer. It makes perfect sense to tax every shot and compensate the afflicted from that fund. That can only happen with people power. If the vaccine figures fall below 80 per cent and mothers hold back, that will happen. It will be a small comfort if your child is harmed. I am working with Brussels, with Gay Mitchell and Commissioner John Dalli, who is responsible for the health and safety of children, to achieve that law for all of Europe.

———

This has been a horrendous task for me, to go back over my life and get this book to every mother possible. I do not know what will happen to me in the future: will this terrible multiple sclerosis get worse or will they find a cure? God knows, medicine owes me my life back. I am sure that readers will be thinking, how does she cope? I have four wonderful children—Tracey, Olga, Karl and Kevin—also a huge circle of wonderful poker players: all 600 of them! I play when I need to escape. There are times when I can laugh so much the tears roll down my face. To all of you, I could not buy what you have done for me over the past ten years.

HOW ALAN DUFFY DIED

This is an itemised documentation of the events in Alan Duffy's life. Everything written here has a matching source document to support each statement.

MARTIN DUFFY

BIRTH AND EARLY MONTHS OF LIFE

Alan Bernard Duffy was born on 11 May 1973 in Mount Carmel Hospital, Dublin, to parents Kevin and Vera Duffy. All records from the time show that it was a normal birth and that he was a healthy baby.

The district nurse, P. Horgan, records that Alan was developing normally: 'Infant thriving', she writes of her first visit on 21 June 1973.

Statements from Vera and Kevin recall Alan's development. Alan's grandmother had nicknamed him 'smiler'. Various relatives recall him as a cheery child, and Vera recalled how 'at evening time he was always in great form and I would love to lie on my back and play with him to tire him out. He was starting to make sounds and laugh out loud.'

Photographs show Alan smiling. One shows him lying on his tummy on a sofa holding up his head and smiling. Another shows him sitting propped up on the sofa. There were no concerns expressed about Alan or his development in these early months of his life.

'Visited frequently and infant found to be progressing normally', the district nurse wrote.

Significant to later events, the district nurse noted of Alan: **21 November 1973 'infant sitting in pram with pillows and support'.**

——

THE UNKNOWN VACCINE DANGERS FACING ALAN

Glaxo Laboratories, makers of the 'triple antigen' (Diphtheria, Tetanus, Pertussis) vaccine, kept records of 'neurological events occurring after administration' of the vaccine. Recorded effects, from the early 60s onwards, were mainly 'convulsions'—usually within hours and sometimes within days of a vaccination—some of which led to death; 'pyrexia' (extremely high temperature); 'encephalopathy' (disease of the brain); and 'cot deaths'.

Professor Gordon Stewart of Glasgow University's Department of Community Medicine also kept records listing convulsions, encephalopathy and coma caused by the pertussis vaccine.

In September 1969, in Cork, baby Kenneth Best began to receive his set of three-in-one vaccinations. It was later proved in court that the batch he received was toxic and caused him lifelong brain damage.

The following month, in Kildare, baby Angela Convey received the first of her set of three vaccinations. She was brain damaged. Professor Conor Ward of Our Lady's Hospital for Sick Children wrote to her mother in 1971: 'It would be unnatural if you did not feel greatly distressed by the fact that the injections which were necessary for your baby's protection against whooping cough and other diseases in fact caused a progressive condition from which recovery was not likely.'

When Angela's father sent a copy of Ward's letter to B. O'Donnell, Kildare County Medical Officer, his letter in reply stated: 'It would serve no purpose for you to report Angela's death to the Eastern Health Board because Our Lady's Hospital Crumlin is an independent voluntary hospital and the Eastern Health Board has no direct control over it.' **In other words, the Medical Officer saw no need to draw attention to a case of vaccine damage and a risk to children.**

In the year of Alan's birth there was much activity regarding the DPT (Trivax) vaccination. In April 1973 the National Drug Advisory Board agreed to a request from Dr A.H. Griffith, head of the Department of Clinical Immunology at the Wellcome Research Laboratories, for clinical trials of a new DPT vaccine in Ireland.

The aim of the research, as written in Dr Griffith's 'protocols for clinical trial' set out in October 1972, was to find a less reactogenic version of the pertussis element of the vaccine. New and current versions of the plain and absorbed vaccines were to be tested.

The trials were carried out by Prof. Irene Hillary. These trials, when details were revealed many years later, were to prove highly controversial in terms of their ethics: orphans were part of the trial group. Worse still, it later transpired that animal vaccine (Tribovax) was mistakenly being used in Ireland around this time, and some of this was used in Prof. Hillary's trials.

Wellcome issued a press release in July 1997 regarding the trials. In it they said the trials were initiated because of 'an increase in reports of the level of adverse reactions among vaccinated children in Dublin'. In that statement it said: 'There would have been medical awareness and the Company had warned that DPT vaccinations can cause side effects, e.g. sore arms, fever and irritability.'

This statement fell far short of the truth. It made no mention of the convulsions—some resulting in deaths—encephalopathy, pyrexia and cot deaths Wellcome had itself been documenting.

These trials were under way by June 1973 when 14 children were immunised at the Madonna House orphanage.

However, there is a set of correspondence between M. Dunlevy, deputy Chief Medical Officer of the Eastern Health Board, and the above mentioned Dr Griffith of Wellcome regarding a rise in reactions to Trivax. The correspondence **begins on 22 August 1973**. The tests being carried out by Prof. Hillary, therefore, must have been in response to concerns expressed prior to this exchange of correspondence. 'These frequent reactions are causing us concern as regards the advisability of continuing Trivax', Dr Dunlevy notes in the letter. She writes of 70 cases within the previous month, stating some had to be admitted to hospital. 'All cases resolved within 4–7 days except two cases of infantile spasm which are still under treatment.' She listed specific batches that were causing concern: 84008, 84769, 84657, 84018 and 84019.

Dr Griffith replied seeking more information. In her reply to that letter, Dr Dunlevy notes: 'I understand that Dr Hillary had mentioned the more severe reactions to you last month. We have some material of batches 84657, 84018 and 84019 which we used in Dr Hillary's survey ...'

Dr Griffith wrote offering to 'send to Dublin a trained nurse competent in the field of clinical investigations'. In this letter he also refers to his records of some Trivax reactions in 1970–73. He refers to two children developing **hypsarrhythmia**, stating also: 'hypsarrhythmia usually develops in children between the ages of 8 and 15 months in both the vaccinated and the non-vaccinated. This coincides with the age at which vaccines are given and since 80 per cent of children are vaccinated, 80 per cent of hypsarrhythmics have a history of vaccination.' This is interesting in that it is typical of the way statistics have later been used to shift any blame from vaccine damage.

NOTE: Hypsarrhythmia is defined as: '*abnormal interictal high amplitude waves and a background of irregular spikes seen in electroencelephogram mostly in infant diagnosed with infantile spasms. They both vary in duration and size, have no rhythm or pattern and can alternate between focal or multifocal. In most cases of infantile spasms hypsarrhythmia disappear during a cluster of spasms and/or REM sleep. In simple terms, it is a very chaotic and disorganised brain wave behaviour with no recognisable pattern, where a normal EEG shows clear separation between each signals and visible pattern. Hypsarrhythmia rarely persists beyond the age of 24 months.*

Dr Dunlevy replied (24 September) and, referring to files she had attached regarding the cases causing concern, she notes: 'We are not so much worried about these from a clinical aspect but they cause considerable damage to the immunisation scheme. Our nurses report that mothers are reluctant and often refuse further immunisation when a child has reacted badly.' Dr Dunlevy declined the offer of a nurse being sent by Wellcome, stating, 'it could possibly raise parental doubts' and states her main purpose in reporting these reactions is to 'seek help from the laboratory service such as the possibility of reducing or altering the pertussis element of the vaccine'.

Concluding this set of correspondence, Dr Griffith writes: 'We hope to have available a less reactive vaccine next year but nevertheless I must attempt to solve the problem of high reactogenicity in Dublin before then.' The letter is dated 2 October: two weeks before Alan Duffy's first DPT injection.

A letter from GlaxoWellcome to Chief Medical Officer Dr James Kiely in October 1997, when the 1970s trials were being investigated, appears to confirm a particular case of concern: 'The batch numbers for the plain control 84019/84657 are mentioned by Dr Dunlevy's report and [document blanked] is cited in both reports.' If this is so then it is a stunning statistic. 116 children were used in the trial. Of these, half received the standard DPT vaccine of the time and half a new vaccine formula with reduced amount of the pertussis element. Yet one child in 116 became seriously ill.

The findings of the trials were never published, but file notes were released for the inquiry. These state: 'The new plain vaccine is the least reactogenic and is likely to be significantly better than all other formulations.... The existing plain vaccine is the most reactogenic and was associated with severe general reactions in two children such that the administration of a second dose was considered unwise.... There is not much to choose between the new and existing absorbed vaccines as far as reactions are concerned. Perhaps the new might be marginally better tolerated but three severe febrile responses were documented following it while none occurred after existing absorbed vaccine.'

Given the proven fact that there were faulty and even animal vaccines in circulation in Ireland from Wellcome around the time of Alan's vaccinations, given the fact that tests were being carried out to try to reduce reactions to the pertussis vaccine, and given the fact that there was particular concern about severe reactions in Dublin, it is reasonable to say that the onus is on GlaxoWellcome to prove to Kevin and Vera Duffy that the batches of vaccine used to inject their son Alan passed all required lab tests for safety.

———

ALAN'S THREE VACCINATIONS

On 17 October 1973, Vera Duffy brought her five-month-old son Alan to the Edenmore Health Clinic for his first vaccination. At that time the CWCS (Community Welfare Clinics) were operating to an 'Immunisation Procedure—Summary' notice issued in September 1973 by deputy Chief Medical Officer Dr M. Dunlevy. It stated, regarding the DPT: 'An infant who has had convulsions may be immunised with three injections of non-absorbed DT after two years of age.' Alan had not experienced convulsions at this stage.

There were no posted signs in the clinic for the public regarding contra-indications. Vera Duffy was not told of any contra-indications regarding Alan's being vaccinated and was unaware of any possible link between epilepsy (from which two of her relatives suffered) and the vaccination. 'I was asked no question about family history illnesses', she stated. However, the doctor who administered the first vaccination wrote in a statement in March 1975: 'As customary I questioned the mother and received no adverse answers and certainly I was told of no family history of epilepsy. In consequence of no adverse conditions being told to me, I proceeded with the innoculations . . .' Interestingly, the 'Immunisation Procedure' notice makes no reference to epilepsy. Given that later epilepsy would be used as the way to explain Alan's condition, this is important to note and keep in mind.

No mention of epilepsy in the family being a contra-indication was listed by the medical officer, but the official publication of the Council of the Pharmaceutical Society of Great Britain, published in 1947, stated of the vaccine:

> though rare, encephalopathies have been noted in association with inoculations of vaccine; American workers now recommend that no child should be injected with large doses of pertussis vaccine if there is a family or personal history of convulsions or if the child has any form of illness pertaining in any way to the central nervous system.

Were the doctors aware of epilepsy in the family of a child as a contra-indication for the vaccine? Was Wellcome? Was the Eastern Health Board? Was this written anywhere? Vera Duffy was not made aware of any such danger. She was not asked if there was a history of epilepsy in her family.

Alan received his first DPT vaccine, batch number 85279.

"Alan cried a lot the night of his first injection," Vera stated. "Over the following days Alan seemed to change for fleeting seconds. He would drain of all colour in his face, turn an ashen grey and his eyes would roll. This lasted for 2/3 seconds culminating with a quick jerk of his arms." Vera had been told not to worry if Alan was irritable after the injection. Within days she called out her local doctor, Dr Kiernan, who said Alan had a slight temperature but there was nothing to worry about.

On 12 December, Vera returned with Alan to the Edenmore Health

Clinic for the next vaccination appointment. She was concerned about how troubled Alan had been after the first injection and tried to have this second injection postponed. However, Dr Maire Kennedy, who gave the injection, stated 'no reaction reported' from the previous injection. Dr Kennedy wrote: 'Was the baby well at that time? Yes. Baby appeared well. Immunisation given.'

Alan received his second DPT vaccine, batch number 85401.

The guidelines from the deputy Chief Medical Officer issued in September still applied, however, and stated: 'An infant who has had convulsions may be immunised with three injections of non-absorbed DT after two years of age.'

Alan should not have received this second vaccination.

Vera states that within a short while of arriving home Alan started to scream and cry. "The jerks of his arms and his face would go grey as before, only more prolonged," Vera stated. After this he also began projectile vomiting his bottle feed. Again the local doctor was called, and again Vera was told there was no need for concern.

On 3 January 1974, Vera brought Alan for his developmental check at the Edenmore Health Centre. The examination was carried out by paediatrician Dr Neil O'Doherty. He records of Alan: 'His performance was not up to the expected standard in the tests applied. He did not sit alone . . . I formed the impression that this was either minor neurological dysfunction of obscure origin or that the boy could be slow within the normal range.' Vera states that she informed O'Doherty of Alan's vomiting and convulsions. Later, in a handwritten note dated 18 April 1974, O'Doherty wrote of Alan: 'Development delay of obscure origin E. hypotonia noted in January.'

'Hypotonia' is defined as '*a condition of abnormally low muscle tone (the amount of tension or resistance to movement in a muscle), often involving reduced muscle strength. Hypotonia is not a specific medical disorder, but a potential manifestation of many different diseases and disorders that affect motor nerve control by the brain or muscle strength*'. Hypotonia would, in other words, describe limpness.

The district nurse noted of a visit to the Duffy home on 10 January 1974: 'Infant was not sitting alone—falling to one side—not grasping objects or taking anything in his hand.'

For whatever reasons, the deputy Chief Medical Officer issued a new notice to 'all immunisation doctors' in January 1974 stating: 'Neurological complications occasionally follow Pertussis vaccine. If you learn that after a previous injection the child was unnaturally limp or drowsy, or had a convulsion or any other sign of Encephalopathy, a further injection must not be given.'

On 6 February 1974, Vera brought Alan to Edenmore Health Centre at the appointed time for his third DPT injection. The doctor was again Dr Maire Kennedy. Vera states: 'I told the doctor how Alan was behaving and what Dr O'Doherty had said. The doctor replied that if Alan does not get his injection he would be a lot worse off.' Dr Kennedy wrote, however: 'Was the baby all right after the first/second immunisations or was there any reaction? No reaction reported on either occasion.'

Despite the reported limpness and convulsions, despite developmental concerns expressed by a specialist, despite concerns expressed by the district nurse and by Alan's parents, despite revised warnings from the deputy Chief Medical Officer referring precisely to these signs, Alan received his third DPT vaccine, batch number 85404.

From this point on, Alan would never be the same again. Vera recalled: "On the way home from the third vaccination, Alan started screeching in the pram—the noise was somewhere between a high-pitched screaming and a grunt. I would later learn to recognise that sound as the start of a convulsion, but I didn't know then what it was. I looked in at him in the pram wondering if he had thrown up. He hadn't. But I rushed home as quickly as I could.

"On that day and the next, Alan was a mass of convulsions. Nothing could settle him and I didn't know what to do. My nine-month-old baby was being taken over by these terrible attacks of shaking and shrieking and going into spasms."

Regarding the third injection,

Where was Alan's medical file when he attended the clinic for his third injection?
Did the vaccinating doctor, Kennedy, refer to Alan's file before giving the injection?
Were Dr O'Doherty's concerns of 3 January noted in Alan's file?
Was the district nurse's concern of 10 January noted in the file?
Were Vera Duffy's concerns ever written into Alan's file?
Was the new January directive from the deputy Chief Medical Officer referred to before considering giving the third injection?
Were Eastern Health Board or Wellcome concerns about vaccine reactions—particularly in Dublin around this time—compared with these concerns about Alan?

A photocopy of Alan Duffy's 'Child Health Service pre-school Card' was sent from Prof. Neil O'Doherty to Chief Medical Officer Dr Brendan O'Donnell in December 1980. Under the section 'Family and Social Factors' there is a subheading 'Relevant family history e.g. chronic illness . . . etc.' No details have been filled in. Under the heading 'Genetic History' nothing has been filled in. Under 'Immunisations', for some reason details of the third vaccination have not been filled in. Under 'Condition at birth' the heading 'Normal' has been ticked.

By April 1974, a *World in Action* programme on ITV had raised the alarm on the dangers of the pertussis vaccine. The deputy Chief Medical Officer, Dr Dunlevy, issued a new directive 'to each immunisation Doctor' in June 1974 regarding 'public anxiety and concern' and added a new alert: 'It is essential to take stringent precautions in history taking before giving any vaccination, especially Pertussis vaccine.'

This had come too late for Alan Duffy, who had already begun his life of suffering in the wake of vaccine damage.

———

ASSESSING THE DAMAGE

In the year following the third vaccination, Alan was examined many times by many doctors and underwent many tests.

District nurse Horgan wrote: 'Special appointment made to see Dr O'Doherty because on visit to home on 21/3/74 infant was still making no attempt to sit up alone and I was not happy about him.'

Dr O'Doherty referred Alan to Dr Ciaran Barry of the Central Remedial Clinic.

Dr O'Doherty also referred Alan to Dr Niall O'Donohoe for an EEG at Our Lady's Hospital for Sick Children.

Alan was also referred to audiologist Sr M. Lydia at Temple Street Children's Hospital.

The medical record on 20 April from the Department of Electroencephalography states: 'Mild development delay—? cause not sitting up' later states 'no interest in things'. Under the heading family history is the scribble: 'No FH ep/conv/MH'—presumably meaning 'no family history epilepsy, convulsions, mental health'.

The result of the EEG, dated 22 April, states: 'Very restless, crying baby. Satisfactory record. A mainly regular and symmetrical pattern predominated throughout.' The conclusion was: 'Normal EEG.'

On 6 May Dr Ciaran Barry wrote of Alan: 'He has good tone, no scissoring and I can find no obvious defects. However, he still cannot sit and has no protective reflexes.'

Sr Mary Lydia, audiologist, wrote on 28 May: 'Alan seemed immature and his responses were certainly immature. However, he responded quite consistently to loud sounds only, with no response to quieter sounds.' Sr Lydia sought a further examination.

An examination at Temple Street Hospital on 7 July, carried out by a Dr J. McAteer, notes nothing in 'family history' about epilepsy. Under 'history of present illness' is listed: 'slight deafness, slow to sit up, reduced co-ordination, difficult to communicate with at times, periodic spasms involving arms-legs-face . . .'

Dr N. O'Donohoe wrote of Alan on 18 July: 'It seems to me that he will be moderately mentally handicapped in the future.'

Dr Ciaran Barry wrote Dr O'Doherty on 29 July: 'I saw this child again after an interval of about 2 months. The mother is very concerned because she says that she has a sister and a first cousin who both suffer from Epilepsy. Because of this, she took the child direct to Niall O'Donohoe in Crumlin. The parents report that an EEG was normal. They also said that Niall said the child was mentally handicapped. I don't know what he said about the epilepsy, but it would seem from the history that the child is having about ten attacks of petit mal per day.'

On 15 August, Dr O'Doherty and Dr O'Donohoe met together with Alan's parents Kevin and Vera. He wrote that Vera 'had also noted some "turns" which we thought might be consistent with Petit Mal and it was said that these had been happening perhaps twice a day since the time the first EEG had been done. It was arranged that a repeat tracing would be done.'

On 15 August, Dr O'Doherty referred Alan to Dr Barbara Stokes of St Michael's House.

Also on 15 August, Dr O'Doherty wrote to Duffy family doctor Kiernan informing him of his referring Alan to St Michael's House 'because it looks as if he will have a mild educational problem that they can best deal with'.

On 22 August, Sr Lydia wrote stating: 'If he has any hearing loss it is very mild indeed.'

On 21 October, a second EEG was carried out. The report states: 'The record showed a marked deterioration since the previous tracing. Almost continuous high voltage bilateral spike discharges were present.' The conclusion was: 'The record shows very frequent generalised epileptic disturbances.'

Notes on a medical examination of Alan at St Michael's House on 22 November 1974 under 'diagnosis' states: **'Deterioration (arrest?) of motor development since 6/12 old ?triple vaccine?'**

By March 1975 Sr Lydia had concluded: 'It seemed that even if there was hearing loss it was not a major problem', and she continued: 'Alan may be simply ignoring sound.'

On 2 March 1975, however, the *Sunday Press* had an article about Kevin and Vera and their child Alan who they believed had been brain-damaged by the pertussis vaccine.

Once Kevin and Vera went public about their belief that Alan had been brain-damaged by the vaccine, the medical profession would deny this possibility by stating that Alan was in fact epileptic. Yet none of the following symptoms noted in Alan are symptoms of epilepsy:

Development delay
Not sitting up
No interest in things
No protective reflexes
Difficult to communicate with
Deterioration (arrest?) of motor development since 6/12 old
Ignoring sound

Alan was described by his parents and by doctors as 'withdrawn'. Is this a symptom of epilepsy?
    The fact that the first EEG showed normal begs the question: what was causing the regression in Alan that his parents and the doctors were seeing and noting?

An undated (post January 1975) document on 'Child Development and Assessment Clinic, Ballymun Road' headed paper gives Dr Barbara Stokes's appraisal of Alan. In her summary she states: 'There is no doubt the child is now suffering from epilepsy, and there is no evidence that the immunisation procedures were in any way connected to this problem, nor is there evidence the child was normal at 6 months, sitting supported etc.'

This is incorrect. Aside from statements from Alan's parents and relatives, the district nurse (see above) noted of six-month-old Alan: **21 November 1973 'infant sitting in pram with pillows and support'.**

At the end of Dr Stokes's appraisal is a handwritten addition: 'Telephone communication with Niall O'Donohoe today. He thinks there can be no charge of neglect by CWC as the 1st description of hypsarrhythmia following triple vaccine was not published until Jan. 1974. This child was immunised in 1973.'

This is incorrect. Alan's last injection was in February 1974. Obviously, however, Dr Stokes was addressing concerns about legal action regarding Alan's treatment and condition.

In what appears to be an earlier draft of this medical report, Dr Stokes notes the dates of Alan's three vaccinations. She notes Alan's 'retardation of gross motor development' and that 'during this period, immunisation procedures were carried out by Edenmore Clinic'.

NOTE: this is further evidence that at least the third vaccination should not have been given if the health professionals responsible for Alan were keeping proper track of his case.

Dr Stokes notes that 'Gross motor development still retarded in January 75. No development of a parachute reflex', and adds in handwriting, 'now epileptic'.

NOTE: then what was the source of Alan's illness and symptoms before this stage of being 'now epileptic'?

In a handwritten addition at the end of this report, Dr Stokes writes: 'telephone communication with Niall O'Donohoe. John Wilson published 1st description Jan 74 of hypsarrhythmia follow triple vaccine'.

NOTE: Alan's third injection was given in February 1974, and Dr Stokes appears to again be concerned about the chronology of the dates of vaccinations and publishing of new information about vaccine dangers.

From the third vaccine onwards, Alan's fits and convulsions had become more frequent and more extreme and his development deteriorated. He had been brain-damaged for life by the pertussis vaccine.

———

THE CASE GOES PUBLIC

A government document of May 1974 released to Vera under the Freedom of Information Act presents a response to a *World in Action* TV programme at that time about the pertussis vaccine. The document noted: 'Dr Dunlevy said it had been found that there was a reaction to certain batches of vaccine and investigations showed that these batches had not been used in Great Britain.'

An article in *The Irish Times* on 27 September 1974 reported on an event that was part of the medical postgraduate week. At a seminar (sponsored by the vaccine manufacturer Wellcome), a Dr Freestone of Wellcome argued for a systematic compensation programme for vaccine-damaged children. This was supported by the doctors and specialists present. To quote the article: 'Brain damage did occur—even if the incidence was rare—and Dr Freestone made recommendations on how doctors could avoid these serious complications.'

When Alan's story reached the newspapers it very quickly became a political issue with questions raised in the Dáil. In a 'note for Tánaiste from Mental Health and Services for the Handicapped Division', the following information was stated about Alan: 'In a child who develops encephalitis following vaccine symptoms of convulsion, stupor and pyrexia develop shortly after vaccination. In this child's case no such symptoms were noted, or mentioned by the parents.'

This is incorrect: The parents had indeed been expressing concern and reporting Alan's illness. Indeed, before the third vaccination, the district nurse, the paediatrician, the Eastern Health Board (in its January directive) and the parents were all expressing concern.

The note continues: 'A report dated 21 October 1974, some nine months after the completion of the vaccination course, indicates that the child was suffering from epilepsy.'

This begs the question: What had been causing Alan's other symptoms and his deterioration over the previous almost full year?

In a document titled 'Note for the Minister' in the wake of the March 1975 newspaper article about Alan, under the heading 'Views of Medical Chief Officer' is stated: 'Like many vaccines pertussis vaccine can cause reactions and there is some evidence that on rare occasions it may cause more serious reactions affecting the central nervous system; but the subcommittee had taken the view that it was difficult to pin down what were the specific dangers of the whooping cough vaccine and concluded that there was no evidence that it was more dangerous than other vaccines.'

In a note regarding a draft of the above document, deputy Chief Medical Officer James H. Walsh writes: 'I would bring out the point that CMOS have reported a drop in vaccination levels over the past 12 months due to this scare and that the 1st quarter of this year has shown an increase in the number of cases of whooping cough (mention number of deaths).'

A further briefing for the Minister under the heading 'possible supplementary questions' advises: 'If the minister is pressed about the particular case referred to in the report it is suggested that he should stress the lack of any report on adverse reactions to pertussis vaccination and say that there is no evidence before him to indicate that the child is mentally handicapped as a result of vaccination.'

When the Tánaiste and Minister for Health, Brendan Corish, answered questions on the issue in the Dáil on 11 March 1975 he stated, as per advice given, that the drop in vaccination rates as a result of the controversy had led to 'an increase in the number of cases notified and two deaths from the disease were recorded in the first three quarters of 1974'. He also stated: 'It is difficult to discern between chance-associated reactions and vaccine-attributable reactions in infants. Vaccinations are not compulsory.'

On 13 March 1975, the district nurse, P. Horgan, submitted her 'Special Report on baby Duffy' quoted at times above. She notes that of 17 January 1975: 'On this home visit mother told me for the first time that there was a strong history of epilepsy in her family.'

This begs the question: Didn't the nurse ever ask Vera about her family medical history? Wasn't there any questionnaire or any

working method to process a new baby's medical profile? The onus was not on Vera to know whether or not her family medical history was relevant to the vaccination process.

The Association for Vaccine-Damaged Children had gathered reports from the many people who had approached Vera Duffy after the newspaper articles about Alan appeared. These reports were sent to the Minister for Health. He responded in February 1976 through a letter from his representative P.W. Flanagan: 'The conditions to which the reports relate can be the result of one or more of a number of different causes. The information furnished in the reports does not establish that the condition of any of the children was the outcome of vaccination.'

By May 1977, however, the Minister decided to set up an 'independent group of medical experts' and wrote to the Association asking 'to meet representatives of your Association for discussions regarding the composition of the Group'.

In a new government, Minister for Health Charles Haughey set up the Group. The Association for Vaccine-Damaged Children did not take part in this as they felt the panel was not impartial. It was headed by the Dublin Chief Medical Officer, Brendan O'Donnell.

This was the same 'B. O'Donnell' who, as Kildare County Medical Officer, told Angela Convey's father (letter quoted above) that 'it would serve no purpose for you to report Angela's case to the Eastern Health Board'.

In August 1982, the decisions of this panel of experts were finally made public. Fourteen cases were told they could receive £10,000 but could not seek further compensation, although Minister Woods stated, 'there is no conclusive evidence that the vaccination caused the disability in any of the persons'.

The experts could say that Noel Thornton was not damaged by the vaccine. Noel was a perfectly healthy child of a year and ten months— talking, playing football—when he was given his first vaccination. That night he was having screaming fits. The doctor gave him the following two vaccinations despite the protests of his father, and Noel ended up dumb, near blind and paralysed. At first the diagnosis was polio, but this was later changed to encephalitis (which is defined as an acute inflammation of the brain commonly caused by viral infection).

Another rejected case was that of Patrick O'Halloran. The hospital where he was born attested to the fact that he was perfectly healthy until he had the vaccine, and the doctor who administered the vaccine wrote a letter saying she believed the vaccine was the cause of his brain damage.

Before the issue of vaccine damage became front page news in Ireland, it had been considered in medical circles that such damage happened, that compensation should be granted to the children damaged and that a safer pertussis vaccine should be found. Once it became a matter of public concern and a political issue, all efforts were made to downplay the damage and to avoid attributing any case to vaccine damage. Even if the principle of damage was grudgingly accepted, experts refused to accept a causal link between specific damaged children and the vaccine.

———

POST-PERTUSSIS BRAIN DAMAGE

On 14 April 1975, Alan had a further EEG. The report described him as a 'quiet, withdrawn child, who slept for part of the record'. The conclusion was: 'the record shows marked improvement compared with the tracing of October 1974, but there are still epileptic discharges present during sleep. The record does not present any of the changes of hypsarrhythmia.'

There was a further EEG test on 9 July 1975. It again described Alan as a 'withdrawn, fairly quiet child'. It stated that 'no definite epileptic features were seen clinically'. It concluded: 'The record is generally dysrhythmic and shows frequent epileptic discharges. The pattern is not, however, one of hypsarrhythmia now.'

The deterioration and withdrawal that had been concerning Alan's parents since he was six months old was continuing. On 23 September 1975, a psychological assessment stated: 'Alan's functional level is less than the 3-month level.'

A medical report written in October 1975—apparently by Dr Stokes—comments: 'All primitive reflexes have disappeared', and later, 'his muscle tone is altering slowly from being an extremely floppy hypertonic infant and now appears to have an increasing rigidity of his upper limbs'. Also, 'The anti-epileptic drug Rivitril, which is at present being given to the child, is being reduced in an attempt to identify existing epilepsy if it is present.'

The conclusion of the report stated: 'Alan is now presenting as a severely mentally handicapped child, with delayed development which, in my opinion, does not seem to have altered in the last 6 months. He does not have grand mal major epileptic attacks. No reasons for the development delay and mental handicap have been elicited.'

NOTE: Again it is being stated that '**No reasons for the development delay and mental handicap have been elicited.**'

In March 1976, Alan was referred at Vera's request to senior consultant neurologist Dr John Wilson at the Hospital for Sick Children, Ormond Street, London. Dr Wilson was mentioned (see above) in a Dr Stokes note as having reported cases of hypsarrhythmia after triple vaccine. In his medical report on Alan, Dr Wilson summarised the events and symptoms in Alan's case. His opinion was: 'Alan is severely mentally handicapped and suffers from myoclonic epilepsy. He may have suffered from infantile spasms as well as major fits in the past. The circumstantial evidence suggesting that his condition results from encephalopathic complications of DPT vaccine, of which the pertussis component is strongly suspect, is strong. There is now no effective treatment for this condition . . .'

For the first time, a medical professional expressed the view that Alan was, indeed, damaged by the pertussis vaccine.
Below are other times when this cause was stated.

On 24 September 1976, Alan was in Temple Street Hospital 'under the care of Prof. O'Doherty'. On one page of the medical file is written: '**NB became retarded after whooping cough vaccine. Epilepsy on Epilim 100 mgs.**'

Later on the same medical file is written: '**Retarded post pertussis vaccine.**'

A doctor's referral note of 21 March 1977 describes Alan as '**a 4½ yr old vaccine damaged child with very frequent convulsions**'.

Dr Stokes, in a referral letter on 18 April 1977 for Alan to Dr Michael Mulcahy of Stewart's Hospital, Palmerstown, writes: 'This child is a hipso rhythmia with severe/profound mental handicap.'

On 2 June, Dr Stokes wrote again to Dr Mulcahy saying: 'The social worker in the past has not had any real contact with the family, partly as they are private patients and partly as they were causing so many public difficulties.' She later notes: 'I think her (Vera Duffy's) pending litigation has probably coloured the service that she is receiving.' This comment was soon proven correct.

On 11 November 1977, Alan was referred to Dr Niall O'Donohoe at the Children's Hospital Crumlin by Dr Noel O'Donnell of St Michael's House. Dr O'Donnell wrote: '**Alan has a history of ? brain damage from the triple vaccine and in addition has developed epileptic attacks.**' He notes also: 'Over the past 1/12 these attacks have increased in severity and there is concomitant vomiting.'

The medical file for this hospital term, starting 23 November, is headed: 'for investigation of epileptic attacks'. The medical notes state: '**Convulsions started at age of 6/12 after first injection of DPT.**'

However, the following day Dr Niall O'Donohoe writes on the medical file: 'I am not prepared, for many reasons, to take this child on as a patient here. He should be returned to St Michael's House. Not for EEG here.'

In a letter on the same day to Dr Barbara Stokes, Dr O'Donohoe adds: 'I am prepared to see him there (St Michael's House) in consultation with you, but that is as far as I am prepared to go.'

Dr Neil O'Doherty, who had first seen Alan in the Edenmore Clinic in January 1974, wrote of Alan again on 3 April 1978 following Alan's readmission to hospital following a continuous onset of convulsions.

He described Alan as 'this boy with severe development delay of obscure origin together with epilepsy . . .'

NOTE: 'Epilepsy' and 'Severe development delay' are being separately categorised.
On 13 May 1980, Dr O'Doherty wrote to Miss Butler, secretary of the Children's Hospital, Temple Street, stating of Alan Duffy: 'I will not have this boy either as my in-patient or out-patient in this hospital or St Anthony's Hospital ever.'

The above was in response to a request from St Michael's for a place for Alan in St Anthony's while his parents took a holiday.

References to the cause of Alan's condition cropped up from time to time on medical notes. An 'opthalmological report on Alan Duffy' dated 9 February 1983 notes at the top of the page: '**Post pertussis vaccine encephalitis**'.

Alan's health was further deteriorating. A medical report of 5 April 1983 states: 'He is non-ambulant and it has been noted that muscle stiffness is increasing.'

On 4 August 1984, Dr Fintan Harte on behalf of Barbara Stokes referred Alan to the National Children's Hospital, Harcourt Street. In his letter he states of Alan: '**He is severely mentally handicapped following adverse reaction to pertussis immunisation.**'

An undated medical chart (from Alan's St Michael's House files) states under diagnosis: 'Past: **?Encephalopathy**. Present: Epilepsy (myoclonic).' On the following page is written: '? **following 3:1 vaccine—infantile spasm**'. The report describes Alan's 'mental handicap' as 'severe'.

On 23 September 1986, a letter was sent from Mary Heapes, 'Reg to Dr McDonnell' at St Michael's House to Dr Stokes. In the letter she states: 'Many thanks for accepting this young 13 yrs boy **who is mentally handicapped—? due to encephalopathic complications of DPT vaccine**.'

In the same letter, Dr Heapes notes: 'Up to recently his epilepsy was reasonably well-controlled on above meds but in past few weeks his seizure pattern has changed—increased in frequency and severity (grand mal).'

Alan's condition continued to deteriorate. On 1 July 1987, Dr Heapes wrote to Dr Stokes, Consultant Paediatrician, National Children's Hospital, Harcourt Street: 'He has had a problem on and off over the past two years of vomiting and retching over short periods of time.'

There are unsigned medical notes (from Alan's St Michael's House file) headed 'medical review' dated 25.5.92, by which time Alan was 19 years old. The notes state: '**Severe mental h'cap, intractable epilepsy— following 3:1 vacc**' (there is a mark before this which is *not* a question mark).

This document also notes that Alan had eight seizures in May and these are 'lasting longer'.

Alan's body became weaker and more deformed by his condition. On 29 June 1992, consultant orthopaedic surgeon Frank McManus notes in a letter to St Michael's House: 'The only thing that's going to change Alan's foot shape is surgery. He is non ambulator and I am not sure that it's warranted.'

Alan's physical condition deteriorated further. On 26 November 1992, Dr Jean Lane writes to Dr McManus: 'The X-rays show bi-lateral dislocation of the hips which is complete on the right side.'

A 'three monthly review' for January to March in 1995, the last year of Alan's life, noted: 'January: 22 seizures. February: 14 seizures. March: 10 seizures.'

After Alan's death, a final entry was made in his St Michael's House file describing the condition of the 22-year-old man before his death: 'Cannot feed self, needs to be fed. Cannot walk, needs wheelchair or buggy. Toileting: dependent. Shows no understanding of words or signs/gestures. Does not use words or signs consistently or meaningfully. Normal vision. Continuous severe or profound hearing loss. Has fits once a week or more often. Needs significant non-invasive care or intervention. Needs extra supervision within a group.'

Which of the above ailments, aside from seizures, can be attributed to epilepsy?

On 15 May 1997, Dr John Wilson provided a revised report to Dublin coroner Brian Farrell with regard to an upcoming inquest establishing Alan Duffy's cause of death. Dr Wilson slightly altered his opinion from

1976, stating in the conclusion of his report: 'It is my opinion that there is strong prima facie evidence indicating that Alan Duffy did suffer adverse reactions to triple vaccine, reactions to which he was predisposed by virtue of having an intrinsically progressive/ degenerative neurological illness which had not yet declared itself at the time of his first injection.'

Dr Wilson did not give his reasons for changing his medical opinion. In March 1976 he concluded, as stated above, that 'the circumstantial evidence suggesting that his condition results from encephalopathic complications of DPT vaccine, of which the pertussis component is strongly suspect, is strong.' In 1997 he changed his opinion on Alan's case despite having had no involvement with Alan in later years. He still states, however, that the vaccine triggered Alan's lifetime of suffering.

NOTE: If there were contra-indications for Alan receiving the pertussis vaccine (for example, epilepsy in two relatives), then of course he was 'predisposed' to adverse reactions. Also, Dr Wilson notes the reaction had not declared itself 'at the time of his first injection'. **But by the second—and particularly the third—concerns from family and even the medical profession itself were being ignored.**

Throughout his medical history, Alan Duffy was diagnosed as having two illnesses: epilepsy and mental handicap of 'obscure' or '?' origin. The origin, however, was clearly, as some members of the medical profession stated, the pertussis vaccine.

He should not have been given the first pertussis vaccine, and it would not have happened if his family medical history had been properly reviewed.

It was wrong to give him the second vaccine when warning signs were already being reported.

And, most particularly, it was a massive failure on behalf of the health professionals responsible for Alan that he was given the third vaccination in February 1974.

Alan's life in the wake of the vaccine damage was one of suffering

caused directly by that damage. He suffered and died as a result of the damage caused by the vaccination. For the sake of justice and for the benefit of all children, this should be acknowledged.

BOOKS AND WEBSITES FOR FURTHER INFORMATION

The Truth about Vaccines by Dr Richard Halvorsen, 2007. This book gives a comprehensive history and overview of vaccines.

A Shot in the Dark by Barbara Loe Fisher and Harris Coulter, 1991. This book from the US deals specifically with the risks involved in the DPT vaccine.

The Vaccine Guide by Randall Neustaedter, 2002. This acupuncturist and doctor of Oriental medicine provides an overview of vaccines, their risks and the alternatives.

Helen's Story by Rosemary Fox, 2006. This is Rosemary's account of her battle on behalf of her daughter and other vaccine-damaged children.

Evidence of Harm: Mercury in vaccines and the Autism Epidemic by David Kirby. The book that set off the controversy about the link between the mercury preservative in vaccine and the rise of autism.

Mother Warriors by Jenny McCarthy. The stories of women who, through diet and other means, have helped their children to recover from vaccine-caused autism.

The River: A journey to the source of HIV and AIDS by Edward Hooper. A heavily researched book that proposes that HIV was man-made, caused by the use in Africa of experimental vaccines contaminated with monkey viruses.

The Vaccine Book: Making the right decision for your child by Robert Sears MD. A doctor's advice on vaccines, including alternative schedules for vaccinations.

The Vaccination Bible by Lynn McTaggart. A highly recommended overview of vaccines and of the general debate about child vaccination.

The internet has brought a boom in information about vaccines. Below are a few of the many sites offering views and updates.

http://www.jabs.org.uk/
This is JABS—the UK support group for vaccine-damaged children.

http://www.vaccinedamage.org.uk/
This is the website of Rosemary Fox's organisation in the UK.

http://www.cryshame.com/
This website is mainly for opponents of the MMR vaccine.

http://www.nvic.org/
This is the website of the National Vaccine Information Center in the US.

http://www.immunisation.ie
This is the Irish government website, from the HSE, giving all its views and guidelines on vaccinations. Needless to say, it dismisses any parental concerns about vaccine damage.